MOUNTAIN	EARTH	WIND/WOOD	FIRE	LAKE
26 Carriage	11 Mirror	Kettle	Treasure	Proclamation
27 Jaws	24 Return	42 Coin	21 Law	17 Leader
4 Child	7 Army	59 Ship	64 Dawn	47 Shadow
52 Silence	15 Monk	53 Seeker	56 Traveler	31 Lover
23 Laundry	2 Cave	20 Tower	35 Prince	45 Council
18 Ghost	46 Growth	57 Prayer	50 Cauldron	28 Peacock
22 Celebration	36 Mask	37 Family	30 Archangel	49 Revolution
41 Pruning	19 Path	61 Falcon	38 Stanger	58 Piper

THE
CELESTIAL
DRAGON
I CHING

THE
CELESTIAL
DRAGON
I CHING

A Unique New Version of the Chinese Oracle for
Making Decisions and Discovering Your Destiny

NEYMA JAHAN

WATKINS PUBLISHING
LONDON

CONTENTS

FOREWORD

First the sky opened ... then the Celestial Dragon was born

The Dragon, the Storm, the Child, the Celebration, the Peacock, the Lover – all these, and more, comprise a repertoire of symbols, each with its own narrative, offering a key to our destiny.

Passing the profound wisdom of ancient China through the prism of a modern Western mind and language, the Celestial Dragon I Ching is designed to be as clear to an English-speaking reader as the original Chinese work would have been to a Chinese reader.

In the ancient Taoist philosophy on which the I Ching is founded, all living beings are animated by energy (*qi*, pronounced "chee"), which consists of two balancing forces, the *yin* (feminine) and the *yang* (masculine). The I Ching maps out the interactions between these two forces, and helps us to understand how they influence our lives, through a simple process that has survived for several thousand years.

The idea is to build up a six-line symbol, known as a hexagram, the interpretation of which will help to guide your actions in relation to the question in your mind at the time of casting the hexagram. There are 64 different hexagrams, each of which comprises a unique permutation of broken lines (representing yin) and unbroken lines (representing yang) and denotes a unique interplay of yin and yang energies.

The Celestial Dragon I Ching provides interpretations not only of the complete hexagrams but also of the individual "changing lines" (see page 17) that may be found within them. This is how the I Ching was originally transcribed, with each changing line making up a part of the whole, just as a human body is composed of feet, legs, hands, arms, torso and head. Understanding the significance of the changing lines gives you an extra level of insight that will greatly enrich your experience of the I Ching.

The world is always the same yet forever changing. And as the world changes, we need to adapt to confront new challenges. For this purpose, I humbly offer you the Celestial Dragon I Ching.

Best of Luck!
Neyma Jahan

INTRODUCTION

The I Ching past and present

According to ancient Chinese tradition, the I Ching was revealed to Fu Xi, the legendary first emperor of China. One version of the story has Fu Xi encountering a mighty dragon, which reared up at him from the waters of the Yellow River. On its back were inscribed eight trigrams (three-line symbols). Fu Xi immediately drew them in the sand with his finger and then, according to some versions, set about pairing them up to form the 64 hexagrams of the I Ching. This was a painstaking and lengthy process, which resulted in what he believed to be a mathematical model of the universe that took account of the complex movements, relationships and changes of all the elements under heaven. Mindful of the significance of Fu Xi's discoveries, his ancestors handed down the hexagrams through generations by oral tradition until, at the dawn of writing around 5,000 years ago, they were inscribed on bones that became known as "oracle bones".

The next major stage in the evolution of the I Ching came in the 11th century BC with the reinterpretation and reorganization of the hexagrams by King Wen, the founder of the Zhou Dynasty (1046–256 BC), and one of his sons, the Duke of Chou. The modern-day I Ching follows the order established at this point, which is consequently known as the "King Wen sequence". Wen and his sons used the wisdom they derived from the hexagrams to plan their successful campaign to usurp the cruel Zhou Xin, the last emperor of the Shang Dynasty (1600–1046 BC).

THE CELESTIAL DRAGON

Whereas Western culture often views the dragon as a symbol of destructiveness and evil, in Chinese myth and legend the creature can be a source of benevolence, wisdom and protection. It became an imperial emblem, and the Chinese emperors sat on the Dragon Throne. As well as having a manifest role in the mythical transference of the I Ching from heaven to Fu Xi (see page 7), the dragon also conveys the I Ching in a more subtle, symbolic way. With its constant coiling and uncoiling, suggestive of retreating and advancing, the creature embodies the Taoist principle of *wu wei* – "effortless action" – which is at the heart of the I Ching.

Five centuries later, the great sage and philosopher Confucius (551–479 BC) added extensive commentaries to the King Wen version, and the I Ching became one of the "Five Classics", the founding texts of Confucianism.

This is the traditional account of the development of the I Ching. Recent archaeological discoveries have led to an alternative theory that the hexagrams and their interpretations were built up from a wider variety of sources during the first stage of the Zhou Dynasty, the Western Zhou period (1046–771 BC).

Whatever the truth of its origins, the I Ching's influence is as powerful as ever today, and indeed has spread from China all over the world. Among the book's most important proponents in the West was the Swiss psychologist Carl Gustav Jung (1875–1961), who in 1949 wrote a famous foreword to the English edition of Richard Wilhelm's translation into German. Jung used the term synchronicity to distinguish the workings of the I Ching from the causality ("if x does y, then the result will be z") that prevailed in Western thought. He helped readers to appreciate that every occurrence of a hexagram is inextricably linked to the moment at which it is cast.

Traces of the I Ching can be found in Jung's own work with archetypes, the universally understood symbols that illuminate the collective unconscious. In the arts, notable figures such as the writers Hermann Hesse and Philip Pullman and the composer John Cage have used the system to create their works. George Harrison wrote the Beatles song "While My Guitar Gently Weeps" after being inspired by the I Ching and then chancing upon the words "gently weeps" in another book.

Preparing for a reading

When preparing to take an I Ching reading, it is essential that your mind is free from distractions and fully focused on the matter on which you are seeking guidance. If you have another subject in your mind while you are casting, the resulting hexagram(s) may relate more to this other subject than the issue you intended to ask about. By centering yourself, you will be able to read the hexagram(s) from an unbiased viewpoint, accepting and understanding what is being told to you rather than unwittingly twisting the reading so that it says what you would like to hear.

There are a number of ways in which you can achieve a settled and focused state of mind. You will know what works best for you, but overleaf are some suggestions:

If you have certain routine tasks – anything from paying bills to doing the dishes – weighing on your mind, it is advisable to get these out of the way before consulting the I Ching. Similarly, tidying the room in which you are going to take the reading may help to unclutter your mind.

Meditation is an age-old method of focusing the mind – for relaxation or spiritual contemplation. The step-by-step exercise opposite adapts the principles of meditation to the I Ching.

Like me, you may like to perform your reading as a ritual. Standardizing the procedure in this way becomes a form of active meditation in itself. I wrap my I Ching book, coins and logbook (see page 24) in a special black woollen cloth and store it above eye level, so that they are protected from any external energetic influences. When I am taking a reading, I unwrap the cloth and use it as a "ground cover" to prevent the book from coming into contact with the floor and absorbing energy from other people's footprints. Contamination of this kind could lead to the result being skewed by the preoccupations of other people. (For this reason it is preferable to take a reading when you are alone – or, if you are taking a reading for someone else, to ensure that the other person is not accompanied by a third party.)

Choosing the coins

The simplest way to cast a hexagram is by tossing three coins six times. Any three coins will do, but many practitioners of the I Ching use coins that have special meaning for them – perhaps ones minted in a significant year or from a significant country. Personally, I use one coin each from the United States, Thailand and Argentina, as I have felt truly at home in each of these places. Decide what is best for you and choose accordingly.

Formulating the question

You will receive the answer you want from the I Ching only if you
ask it the right question. To get the best from the I Ching, the
question should relate to an issue with which you feel emotionally
involved – perhaps a career dilemma or a crossroads in a relationship.
If you ask about a trivial matter, your mind will most probably wander
to more pressing concerns during the casting, which will make the
significance of the reading hard to ascribe.

I CHING MEDITATION

To perform this meditation, you will need
an image of the circular *taijitu* symbol,
commonly known as the "yin-yang" symbol.

1 Sit in a comfortable position, with the *taijitu* symbol in front of
you. Close your eyes and focus on your breathing, which should
be relaxed and uncontrolled.

2 Direct your awareness to the rising and falling of your abdomen.
Don't worry if other thoughts enter your mind: just acknowledge
them, then gently return your attention to your breathing.

3 After about five minutes, slowly open your eyes and begin to
contemplate the *taijitu* symbol. Follow the contours of the
interlocking halves of the emblem. Sense the harmony of the yin
and yang energies operating within your body – the receptive,
yielding yin counterbalancing the creative, forceful yang.

4 When you feel ready, bring your awareness to the question
you wish to ask the I Ching and prepare to throw the coins
(see page 14).

Think deeply about the issue in order to decide on the precise nature and wording of the question. Taking the time to reflect on a significant concern is in itself a valuable exercise.

Remember that the I Ching should be treated as a wise confidant, not as a fortune-teller: it will not tell you what is going to happen. The most powerful results come from asking for understanding or advice. Say, for example, that you are considering applying for a new job. Do not ask, "If I apply, am I going to get this job?", because the answer to this question depends on factors beyond your control. You could ask, "Should I apply for this job?", which would, at least, move the focus of the question to your own actions. However, it is best not to ask directly what to do, but rather to ask for guidance. (Also, closed questions like this one are to be avoided, because the I Ching deals in images: it cannot answer "yes" or "no".) The I Ching teaches us strategy; it knows that everything is possible given the right approach from us, and thus will guide us to decide for ourselves on the correct course of action or non-action. Therefore, a more fruitful way to phrase your inquiry would be: "What if I apply for this new job?"

Often we will want to ask for advice about which of two alternative actions to take, or about whether to do something or not to do something. In these situations, you should not include both options in a single question, because it will be impossible to be sure which of the two possibilities the reading is telling you about. Limit your question to one of the options – perhaps the one you are leaning toward. Alternatively, ask about each of the options one after the other, but give yourself time to reflect on the first reading before taking the second.

Once you have worded your question, write it down in your logbook (see page 24). It is important to have the exact question in your mind while you are casting and interpreting the hexagram(s), because even a subtle change in wording can make a big difference.

One last point: do not ask the same question more than once in a short space of time. As Carl Jung observed about the I Ching, "the master speaks but once". If you are finding it difficult to interpret a reading, put it to one side and come back to it with a fresh mind. If you don't like what it seems to be telling you, remember that receiving a warning from the I Ching is a positive experience, as it enables us to rechart our course.

SUMMARY OF DOS AND DON'TS

DO ask for understanding of an unclear situation first:
Ask, *What are the issues involved in training to run a marathon?*
not *How would training to run a marathon hamper my social life?*

DON'T ask what to do:
Ask, *What if I purchase this investment now?*
not *Should I purchase this investment now?*

DO ask for an image of a potential situation:
Ask, *Give me a picture of what it would be like not to be in this relationship?* not *Should I break off this relationship?*

DON'T ask "either/or" questions:
Ask, *What about if I move to the new house?*
not *Should I move to the new house or should I stay put?*

DO ask open-ended questions:
Ask, *How will my travels enrich my life?*
not *Will I make good friends in foreign countries?*

Casting a hexagram

The basic procedure of the I Ching is to toss three coins six times and to convert the outcome of each throw into a line. (Traditionally, yarrow stalks were used but they are harder to come by and the process is more complicated.) The results of the six throws build up a hexagram *from the bottom*, line by line.

The head side of the coins is yang, the tail side yin. The value for tails is 2 and the value for heads is 3. Each toss of the three coins gives you one of the following totals, each of which represents a different type of energy and is denoted by either a broken $\_\_$ or unbroken $\_\_$ line.

CONVERSION CHART

COINS	TOTAL	ENERGY TYPE	LINE	CHANGING?
3 tails	6	old yin	$\_\_$	changing
1 heads + 2 tails	7	yang	$\_\_$	
2 heads + 1 tails	8	yin	$\_\_$	
3 heads	9	old yang	$\_\_$	changing

As you can see in the chart above, a toss of either 3 tails or 2 heads and 1 tails creates a broken line, and a toss of either 1 heads and 2 tails or 3 heads creates an unbroken line. Here is a sample hexagram:

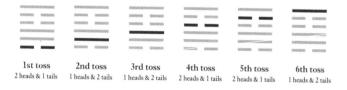

1st toss	2nd toss	3rd toss	4th toss	5th toss	6th toss
2 heads & 1 tails	1 heads & 2 tails	1 heads & 2 tails	2 heads & 1 tails	2 heads & 1 tails	1 heads & 2 tails

The values will soon become second nature, but until they do, use the conversion chart to translate coin tosses into lines of a hexagram.

Each of the 64 hexagrams has a corresponding hexagram number as well as a name. Use the visual index on page 16 to find the hexagram number, which will then lead you to the entry in this book for any hexagram. Find the lower trigram (the bottom three lines of the hexagram) on the vertical axis and the upper trigram (the top three lines of the hexagram) on the horizontal axis. The bottom trigram for the given example is therefore:

and the top trigram is:

Located at the intersection between the relevant row and the relevant column you will find the hexagram in question, represented by a number and name (in this case The Ghost, hexagram 18). Look through this book to find the appropriate hexagram number, then read the corresponding text (The Ghost can be found on page 101). The overall meaning is expressed in the opening paragraph.

Each individual trigram, out of the eight permutations possible, has a meaning in itself, representing an aspect of the universe. These aspects, named in red on the axes of the visual index (page 16), combine with each other to create further, more complex meanings – for example, the three solid lines meaning Heaven, when mirrored to form a double trigram (hexagram), denote The Dragon, the ultimate vehicle of Celestial Power. These trigrams, and their relationships with each other, open up worlds of study in themselves which are explored within the 64 hexagrams.

The 64 Hexagrams: the Visual Index

Use this chart to look up the entry in this book for any hexagram. Find the lower trigram (the bottom three lines of the hexagram) on the vertical axis and the upper trigram (the top three lines of the hexagram) on the horizontal axis. Then find the hexagram located at the intersection between the relevant row and the relevant column.

	HEAVEN	THUNDER	WATER	MOUNTAIN	EARTH	WIND/WOOD	FIRE	LAKE
HEAVEN	1 Dragon	34 Horns	5 Clouds	26 Carriage	11 Mirror	9 Kettle	14 Treasure	43 Proclamation
THUNDER	25 Surprise	51 Alarm	3 Storm	27 Jaws	24 Return	42 Coin	21 Law	17 Leader
WATER	6 Claws	40 Arrow	29 Abyss	4 Child	7 Army	59 Ship	64 Dawn	47 Shadow
MOUNTAIN	33 Hermit	62 Mouse	39 Raven	52 Silence	15 Monk	53 Seeker	56 Traveler	31 Lover
EARTH	12 Bargain	16 Hammer	8 Coven	23 Laundry	2 Cave	20 Tower	35 Prince	45 Council
WIND/WOOD	44 Gate	32 Marathon	48 Well	18 Ghost	46 Growth	57 Prayer	50 Cauldron	28 Peacock
FIRE	13 Beloved	55 Sun	63 Dusk	22 Celebration	36 Mask	37 Family	30 Archangel	49 Revolution
LAKE	10 Razor	54 Servant	60 Dam	41 Pruning	19 Path	61 Falcon	38 Stranger	58 Piper

Changing lines

In the conversion chart (page 14) you can see that throws with all heads or all tails yield what are called changing lines. Changing lines are lines that change from their original broken (yin) lines to unbroken (yang) lines, or vice versa. This means that two hexagrams are created, in turn prompting two complementary readings. The new, additional hexagram that is formed when the changing lines are converted to their opposite (broken or unbroken) is called the "resolved" or "changed" hexagram. Imagine that, in our previous example, our first toss yielded 3 heads (rather than 2 heads and 1 tails): the primary hexagram would be the same, but as the first toss creates a changing line, a new hexagram is also formed (in which an unbroken yang line replaces the original broken yin line):

6th toss	1 heads & 2 tails		
5th toss	2 heads & 1 tails		
4th toss	2 heads & 1 tails		
3rd toss	1 heads & 2 tails		
2nd toss	1 heads & 2 tails		
1st toss	3 heads	✳	

So: *resolves to*

If there are no changing lines, the primary hexagram is your complete answer and you would simply look up the commentary for this hexagram using the visual index on page 16. If, however, a changing line is present you would:

i) begin by looking up the reading for the primary hexagram.

ii) take into account the transforming effect of the changing line and consider the short commentary on that particular changing line.

iii) look up the resolved hexagram and its relevant reading.

In our example, the primary hexagram is The Ghost, 18, page 101, so you would start by interpreting the general reading for this. Next step is to look up the interpretation for the particular changing line you have cast. In this case, it was the first toss that yielded a changing line, so you would need to concentrate specifically on the 1st interpretation, as well as on the general summary. If all six tosses were to give you changing lines, you would use the "all six" interpretation.

As with the first or primary hexagram, use the visual index (page 16) to locate now the relevant entry for the resolved hexagram. In our example it is The Carriage, 26. This complete new hexagram is a third component of your casting, after i) the original hexagram and ii) the changing lines. Hold all three readings in your mind and work on their meaning for you. The primary hexagram represents where we are, the changing line(s) represent what we should do (or not do) and the resolved hexagram represents where we could end up as a result.

Interpreting the hexagrams

The only rule to follow when interpreting the I Ching is to use your intuition. Individual hexagrams do not have a fixed, invariable meaning: their significance will become apparent to you in the light of the circumstances you bring to a casting. The I Ching speaks through metaphor, so you should not take the texts literally. Perhaps certain words, or the images that certain words describe, will jump out at you from the page, triggering a marked response – some kind of echo, signpost, revelation or insight. Intuitively, you will know exactly what to do. What this takes, above all, is a completely open mind: the best results occur when you empty yourself and allow the energies of the I Ching to work on your unconscious.

In this section we will work through a number of examples, starting with the simplest scenario – a primary hexagram with no changing lines – through to the most powerful and unusual reading, a hexagram with all six changing lines.

Single hexagram with no changing lines

Let's say that we are inquiring about what kind of vacation we should go on by asking the I Ching, "Give me a picture of my ideal vacation". We throw the coins and get the scores of 7, 7, 7, 8, 7 and 7, giving us the following hexagram, with no changing lines:

derived from:

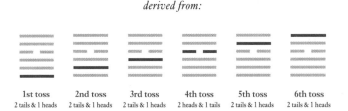

1st toss	2nd toss	3rd toss	4th toss	5th toss	6th toss
2 tails & 1 heads	2 tails & 1 heads	2 tails & 1 heads	2 heads & 1 tails	2 tails & 1 heads	2 tails & 1 heads

Using the visual index on page 16, hexagram 9, The Kettle, is revealed. Since there are no changing lines, the whole of the answer is to be found in the introductory paragraph on page 65:

The kettle sits on the stove, but the water will not boil. Clouds come from the west, but the land remains like a desert; we must drink the tea lukewarm. We will find success in accomplishing smaller things;

as for serious matters, it is advised to wait until another day to move forward.

This seems straightforward: it appears that the I Ching is saying it would be better to wait and organize a vacation later ("another day"). Perhaps some (other?) plan is afoot that requires us to be patient about our trip. The "smaller things" may refer to weekend breaks, or projects to be done in the time we were hoping to be away.

Dual hexagrams with one changing line

Using the same scenario and question, let's say we receive the same hexagram, The Kettle, but with a changing line in the first position so that it transforms into Prayer, hexagram 57 (our first toss yields 3 heads instead of 2 tails and 1 heads):

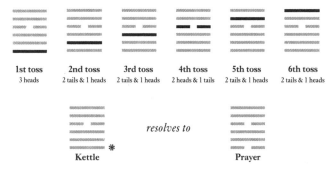

1st toss	2nd toss	3rd toss	4th toss	5th toss	6th toss
3 heads	2 tails & 1 heads	2 tails & 1 heads	2 heads & 1 tails	2 tails & 1 heads	2 tails & 1 heads

resolves to

Kettle   Prayer

Remember: the primary hexagram represents where we are, the changing line(s) represent what we should do (or not do) and the resolved hexagram represents where we could end up as a result.

This time we must take into account not only the opening paragraph for The Kettle, but also the text about the changing line in the first position (page 66):

PURCHASING THE KETTLE – *Scouring the pawnshops, he finds that which he seeks. She sits alone on a dusty shelf and shines with a radiance visible only to his eye. There is praise only for those who stand behind what they love.*

If the changing-line text contradicts what is said in the opening paragraph, this suggests that the I Ching is advising you to take action (represented by the changing line) to change your current situation (represented by the primary hexagram).

The changing-line text in this example refers to something that is "radiant" only to our eye. So perhaps we are being advised to take a vacation to a place not normally frequented by tourists, but somewhere that calls to us personally, reflecting a deep need.

We then move on to the resolved hexagram, Prayer, for which the introductory text reads as follows (page 257):

Prostrating himself before the altar, he submits himself to the will of Heaven. For those who are not religiously inclined, prayer can be taken as a willing submission to a stronger force, much as a woman opens her womb and allows seed to penetrate. Prayer can also mean "to hope" or to let our actions be guided by another, as this is stronger than carrying on alone. We should have a goal or precise request when we pray, and it is advised to take counsel from a wise elder.

So! When we consider this in conjunction with the text for the changing line, we might conclude that if we take a vacation to a quiet place, we will have time to reflect on the inner aspects of our being. There are always many ways to divine a casting. In this case we might be tempted to wonder about the precise meaning of "another" or the "wise elder". But if no interpretation comes naturally we should feel free to ignore such details. The rule is: consider all aspects of the text and then use our intuition, our knowledge of the situation, and any cues from the client to determine the recommended course of action.

Dual hexagrams with multiple changing lines

Often we will cast a hexagram with multiple changing lines. This can get confusing, especially if the meanings of the changing lines appear to contradict each other. Let us look at this example, again beginning with The Kettle, hexagram 9:

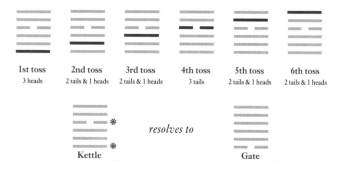

1st toss	2nd toss	3rd toss	4th toss	5th toss	6th toss
3 heads	2 tails & 1 heads	2 tails & 1 heads	3 tails	2 tails & 1 heads	2 tails & 1 heads

Kettle   *resolves to*   Gate

This time we throw a changing line not only in the first position but also in the fourth, giving us the resolved hexagram The Gate, hexagram 44. The text for the fourth line of The Kettle reads:

FILLING THE KETTLE — *Following instructions carefully, he fills the kettle with the correct mixture. Our elders stand in confidence behind us. By following tried and true methods, we will avoid spilling the water.*

The texts for the first and fourth lines seem to contradict each other. The interpretation of the first changing line speaks of searching for something with a "radiance visible only to his eye", so perhaps the reference is to something unconventional; while the fourth line mentions following "tried and true" methods. As always, the key is to use our intuition. Perhaps the two texts are referring to separate aspects of the inquiry. For example, we might guess that the first changing line relates to the location for our vacation, whereas we sense that the fourth changing line relates to the kinds of things we might do while we are there. If you cannot immediately resolve the contradiction, let the reading percolate in your mind and almost invariably you will have a moment of realization at some later time. If all else fails, then the general rule is that the higher, or highest, changing line – in this case the fourth – takes precedence.

Turning now to the interpretation for the resolved hexagram, The Gate, we see how much difference just one extra changing line can make to an overall reading (page 205):

They are drawn to each other upon first sighting as he takes her hand and knows that it is better not to ask her name. This is a time of contact or momentary union. Enjoy it, gain from the experience, using it as a catalyst to draw strength from the source. However, we must not try to make anything lasting, for this path will lead straight into the spider's web.

In contrast with the spiritual contemplation suggested by the Prayer hexagram (see previous example), this resolved hexagram indicates that we will undergo a very intense, but transitory, emotional experience while we are on vacation. Perhaps we will meet someone who makes a deep impression on us – but possibly someone we should never see again.

Dual hexagrams with all six changing lines

Casting a hexagram with all six changing lines should always be taken as a particularly powerful omen. Again using The Kettle as the primary hexagram, the resolved hexagram will be The Hammer, number 16:

Kettle   *resolves to*   Hammer

If this should happen, read the introductory text and all six commentaries on the individual changing lines to obtain a fully rounded understanding of the primary hexagram. However, you should focus mainly on the "all six" commentary:

THE KETTLE EXPLODES – *Unbounded passion rules for but a moment. Experience it, grow from it and then let it go.*

As this is a changing-line text, it is telling us what to do, rather than how things will end up. So, in this instance, perhaps we are being directed to take a vacation with a lover, or go to a place that offers excitement and adventure.

The text for The Hammer, which is the resolved hexagram in this example, reads as follows (page 93):

KEEPING A LOGBOOK

To get the most from the I Ching it is important to record your readings in a logbook. This enables you to study over time how particular readings relate to your later experiences. In the process you will come to understand more about the ways in which the I Ching communicates its wisdom. For each reading make a note of the following details:

– date of the reading
– precise wording of the question you asked
– hexagram(s) cast
– your interpretation of how the text(s) related to you
– what actions you took (or didn't take) as a result
– how the situation in question developed

The hammer strikes the anvil, causing sparks to fly and shaping that which was previously thought unshapeable. The funeral dirge hums as the wise man gathers his resources and prepares to set forth to enact his will. Anything that is solid will be shaped under the pressure of the hammer. But be aware that upon things such as water (the feminine) and wind (the formless) the hammer will have no effect.

Since this is the resolved hexagram, it relates to the outcome of the vacation. We might take this to mean that the vacation will cause us to reshape our life in a significant way.

Sample readings

To demonstrate the I Ching at work in a real-life context, I have provided genuine readings from two of my clients (with their permission). Only names and other identifying details have been changed, to protect confidentiality.

Reading 1: Catherine

Catherine is a 34-year-old professional who has been married to Eric for five years. They have a four-year-old daughter. Over the last two years the pressures of career and home responsibilities have left Catherine feeling somewhat estranged from Eric. Although they work together amicably and effectively to run a household and raise their daughter, they seem to have less and less in common with each other and Catherine senses the loss of the initial "spark" of their marriage.

On a recent business trip, Catherine "met someone". There was no physical encounter; however, according to Catherine it just "felt right" being with him. The dilemma for Catherine now, of course, is whether she should pursue this relationship.

Having formulated the question "What if I continue contact with my new friend?", we throw the coins to cast the following hexagrams:

resolves to

Mask   Monk

Before we examine how I interpreted this, let's turn to the relevant texts. First is the opening paragraph of The Mask, hexagram 36, page 173:

Entering into the earth, the fire will be extinguished. The mask is like the eclipse. This is a quiet, perhaps injurious time where it is best to subdue our own power and yield to others. This is a time to conceal who we are and our true intentions by allowing others to take the limelight as we watch patiently from the shadows. To do otherwise would bring harm to ourselves.

Now consider the first changing line:

THE MASK OF DILIGENCE – *Donning the mask, he is forced to fold in his wings and get back to the grotto. There is work to be done and this should be tackled with the utmost attention. This may mean working three days straight, with little pause for food or sleep. The wise man gets done what must be done and ignores others' foolish comments regarding the diligence of his work.*

Lastly, turn to the opening paragraph of The Monk, hexagram 15, page 89:

The first shall be last and the last shall be first. The wise man knows there is a time to shine and a time to whisper. Now is the occasion to practice modesty, to walk very lightly and to leave no trace. The public dislikes that which is full and reveres that which is empty. Working from the small hours of the night through to the glow of the dawn, the monk takes from where there is too much to augment that which has too little.

The first, primary hexagram opens with an ominous image of a fire being extinguished and refers to subduing our own power, yielding to others and concealing our true intentions. I took this to allude to the current state of Catherine's relationship with Eric, with herself in a subordinate role – not necessarily to Eric exactly, but to what they have built together and to the rearing of their daughter.

So this state of extinguishing light is where we begin. The changing line (which suggests how the situation can evolve in relation to what we should or shouldn't do) speaks of diligence and dedicated work and is not so very different from the resolved hexagram, which implies modesty and treading lightly. (This similarity between the changing line and the resolved hexagram often occurs when there is just a single changing line.)

Based on the combination of the changing line and the resolved hexagram, the I Ching in this instance seems to be telling Catherine that instead of making rash emotional decisions it is time to be straightforward, modest and meticulous regarding her potential new relationship.

In practical terms, I took this to suggest that if Catherine is to maintain any contact with her new friend, it should be at a respectful distance so that her relationship with Eric has a chance to evolve naturally.

I told Catherine that I saw the I Ching telling her not to be rash – not to burn any bridges, or jump into anything with haste. I also told her that when couples encounter difficulties in their relationship, if each tries to work through them in a spirit of respect for their own well-being and that of the other person, often the relationship evolves to a place where the parties grow back in touch with each other again or amicably separate. Either of these would be preferable to separating from Eric before giving their marriage a chance to spark back into life.

I cannot say that my reading is the "definitive" interpretation of these hexagrams. Much relies on intuition and a detailed knowledge of the situation. Anyone can claim to be a mystical sage and "tell a person's future" without any input from them, but what I have found is that the more a subject tells me, the more the hexagrams make sense and the more I can tell them in response.

Reading 2: Jeffrey

Jeffrey is a 46-year-old venture capitalist. He has recently been approached by a partnership that is developing a new web-based service. Each partner has invested a significant amount of their own money and time and the website is almost ready to be launched. However, the partnership is running short on capital and needs outside investment to sustain it until it starts to break even.

To Jeffrey, the business model seemed well-thought-out and the partners committed. However, there is always uncertainty when taking a leap into the unknown, and that is why he has come to me.

With the question "What if I make an investment in this new company?" in mind, we cast the following reading:

Cauldron   *resolves to*   Claws

Let's first read the relevant texts. We start by turning to the opening paragraph of The Cauldron, hexagram 50 (page 229):

The cauldron is used to cook the sacrifice or meal for all. It is now time to make hard decisions and give up something we prize for the sake of furthering our cause. We shall give this thing freely and without regret, for this is the only way that it can assist us. A sacrifice is only a sacrifice if it is something that we love. The wise man spends all day preparing a meal and invites the villagers to his home for the offering.

Then we consider the third and fifth changing lines, "The Cauldron's Handles" and "The Golden Cauldron":

THE CAULDRON'S HANDLES – *The handles are missing and we are unable to offer what we have prepared. Sad that such a thing should go to waste. This happened because we spent too much time reminiscing about the past. In the end, rain will come and make everything right.*

THE GOLDEN CAULDRON – *Our past mishaps have been resolved to the point where everything is in better standing than previously. It is time to be persistent, yet civilized.*

And finally the opening paragraph of The Claws, hexagram 6 (page 53):

Dogs will bark while the tiger hunches and bares its claws. The crowd falls silent to observe the ensuing conflict. Attempting the middle passage will bring small success, yet to pursue relentlessly will surely lead to disaster. It is advised to take counsel from a wise elder nearby and not to travel; for this would surely lead to a watery grave.

As you can see here, a simple question has yielded a complex answer with multiple changing lines. When there are two or more changing lines in a reading, sometimes you will find that they conflict with each other (see page 21). However, that does not seem to be the case here.

Looking first at the opening paragraph for the primary hexagram, we see an emphasis on sacrifice and "giving up something we prize for the sake of furthering our cause". It seems that the I Ching is recommending Jeffrey to make the investment. If this were a stand-alone hexagram, with no changing lines, this would be clear. However, the changing lines significantly modify this message.

The third changing line states that "we are unable to offer what we have prepared", which implies that something may prevent Jeffrey from making good on his intention to invest. However, the fifth changing line tells a slightly different story, saying that "past mishaps have been resolved". This may refer to the apparent sticking point suggested in the earlier changing line. So, it seems that the I Ching is highlighting some technical issues that need to be ironed out, after which it will be appropriate to make the investment. However, we are not finished yet, as the potential hexagram still looms.

The Claws hexagram evokes strife and opposition. Occurring as the resolved hexagram, it implies that if Jeffrey were to make this investment, further down the road some kind of conflict would occur.

As always, the answer is not a cut and dried "yes" or "no". The I Ching is not telling Jeffrey "do not invest", but rather it is painting a picture of the potential evolution of the situation if he goes ahead. Although the message of The Claws hexagram appears unequivocally negative, when I looked at it alongside the fifth changing line – particularly its emphasis on being persistent – I did not rule out making the investment. I told Jeffrey that if he was willing to deal with some turbulence along the way, this project could be successful. But if he wanted an investment whereby he could write a cheque, then wait to collect his returns, this proposal would not be right for him.

If we have good self-understanding, we may find that we already know deep down, by intuition, what the I Ching is telling us. However, some situations are black boxes into which we cannot see unaided. In such cases the I Ching will provide us with invaluable illumination. You are holding a gift in your hands – a mirror into the vast unknowable. The I Ching will always be correct in its own way.

THE 64 HEXAGRAMS

The Celestial Dragon I Ching

A NOTE ON GENDER

"He" is used in this version to be true to the original classic
text of the I Ching, but should be read as a unisex pronoun.
"The wise man", similarly, stands in for "the wise person".

A NOTE ON QUOTATIONS

The quotations that introduce each hexagram commentary
(in italics on the opening page) are the author's own version of the
summaries of each hexagram given in the original I Ching.

"Creation bodes supreme success. With perseverance, all that is undertaken shall come to pass."

THE DRAGON

THE POWER OF CREATION

Endless Heaven

Six dragons ride forth and nourish the earth. Clouds burst asunder and bring rain. What is willed shall be, as he walks upon the righteous path and the world reshapes itself around the power of his word. Understand the nature of creation, acting with boldness and without hesitation. Action is favored.

乾 THE DRAGON

FIRST

THE HIDDEN DRAGON
The wise man conceals his light and
retreats to the mountain to turn his
thoughts inward. He is content with the
practice of perfecting himself. He does this
because he must learn to master himself
before he would think to master others.

SECOND

THE EXPOSED DRAGON
Critics spy him upon the road and
analyze his works. In speech he must
now be humble and elusive, and would
do well to take counsel from a wise elder.

THIRD

THE WORKING DRAGON
Shouldering a self-imposed yoke, he
throws himself into the details of his work.
Trouble threatens, but with meticulous
care and by tying up all loose ends he is
able to remain awake through the night
until the danger has passed.

FOURTH

THE LEAPING DRAGON
Although the road may seem dark, now is
the time to leap forward into uncertainty
and put our faith in the tumble of the dice.
If we have sufficient faith, then luck will
be on our side. Wild horses cannot stop us.

FIFTH

THE SOARING DRAGON

He leaves behind those who dwell on land and seeks out his own kind. It is advised to take counsel from a wise elder and to leave behind those who do not support our goals. After arrival, we look up to see that those who also have wings will have followed.

SIXTH

THE EMPTY DRAGON

Although he is righteous in his cause, his power has departed for the time being. Sparks do not ignite, people do not follow and mountains will not move. It is best now to cease action and retreat to a place where we may contemplate the high and low tides of thought and creation.

ALL SIX

THE HEADLESS DRAGON

Like the sperm entering the egg, the dragon merges with the cave, the right with the left in this ultimate act of creation. Both cease to be as the child of dawn incubates and is born into the world. Ultimate success!

"To lead is to follow, to whisper is wisdom. The receptive bears the burden to completion."

THE CAVE

THE POWER OF RECEPTIVITY

Endless Earth

Like the female who opens her womb and allows the seed
to penetrate, we submit to the creative power and willfully
allow our actions to be guided. At first there may be fear
and confusion, but if we remain within the confines of our
garden and gravitate toward those of our own kind, then
in the end we shall rule through submission. The west
and south are favored and we shall achieve what is willed
by the touch of a feather.

 THE CAVE

FIRST

THE CAVE OF ICE
The winter of our heart is approaching.
Days grow shorter, and outwardly not
much may be accomplished. Now we must
rest on the laurels of our acquired merit
and know that what we have stored is
enough to bring us through to the onset
of spring. The wise man acts with caution
and spends frugally.

SECOND

THE SUPPLY CAVE
We were wise to see that the cave was well
stocked before the coming of winter. Now
all we must do is retreat to this shelter and
enjoy what we have prepared. What has
been willed will come to fruition with no
further action on our part.

THIRD

THE CONCEALED CAVE
Like the mistress of the desert who
conceals her beauty behind a veil and rules
her husband through subtle suggestion,
we should hide our cards well and achieve
victory through well-directed whispers in
the dark. Once the suggestion has taken
hold, we may lift our cloak and radiate
our power so as to close the deal.

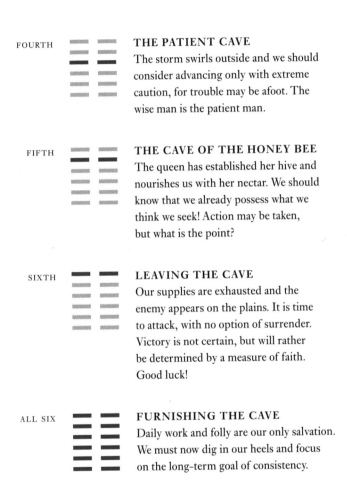

FOURTH

THE PATIENT CAVE
The storm swirls outside and we should
consider advancing only with extreme
caution, for trouble may be afoot. The
wise man is the patient man.

FIFTH

THE CAVE OF THE HONEY BEE
The queen has established her hive and
nourishes us with her nectar. We should
know that we already possess what we
think we seek! Action may be taken,
but what is the point?

SIXTH

LEAVING THE CAVE
Our supplies are exhausted and the
enemy appears on the plains. It is time
to attack, with no option of surrender.
Victory is not certain, but will rather
be determined by a measure of faith.
Good luck!

ALL SIX

FURNISHING THE CAVE
Daily work and folly are our only salvation.
We must now dig in our heels and focus
on the long-term goal of consistency.

*"**Difficulty at the beginning.**
Union of the weak and the strong.
Only after breakthrough shall
order be drawn from confusion."*

THE STORM

THE FURY FROM ABOVE

Water and Thunder

The clouds gather to spit forth thunder and rain. The wise man does not seek to attempt the mountain pass, but rather consolidates his present position and makes preparations for the storm's passing. He who attempts to walk directly into the storm shall find nothing but ruin.

屯 THE STORM

FIRST

SCENT OF THE STORM

The sky may seem clear, but the wind projects ill omen. The wise man does not advance, but rather co-operates with those under his care to consolidate the present position.

SECOND

THE STORM APPROACHES

The hunter is unable to capture the doe. Moisture can be felt in the air. Better to wait, but if he insists on pursuing, he will chase his own tail for ten years, after which she will give her consent.

THIRD

THE STORM BREAKS

The hunter plunged into the forest without a guide and finds himself amidst the torrents. Best now to build a shelter and wait for the sun. Next time he should use more caution.

FOURTH

THE STORM CALMS

The rain stops, but the clouds still hover overhead. Instead of chasing the doe, the hunter lays scent and waits for her willful approach. Good fortune will come by means of patience and righteous intention.

FIFTH

THE STORM DEPARTS
The sky clears and we return to the field
to find that we have planted the wrong
crops. Overwatered! We may pick berries
for sustenance, but attempts to harvest
a ruined field spell disaster.

SIXTH

CASUALTIES OF THE STORM
The hunter returns to his camp to find
his companions are dead and the camp
is in ruins. For three days he will shed
blood and tears, but this too will pass.
In the distance, birds are singing. He
would be wise to release the past and
follow that sound.

ALL SIX

RIDING THE STORM
The hunter jumps onto the back of
danger and rides her to a new land
and a fresh start.

"Seek not, but be sought.
Preservation of character in
the presence of rashness."

4

THE CHILD

BIRTH PAINS

Mountain Stream

We should not seek out the child, nor attempt to give counsel to a deaf ear; rather, it is time to cultivate our own power. Should they come to us asking for assistance, then we slowly begin to divulge our wisdom. If they are impatient and enjoy talking more than listening, then we shall turn a deaf ear to future inquiries. A need for contemplation and proper direction is stressed.

A disciplined education is required.

蒙　THE CHILD

FIRST

THE UNRESPONSIVE CHILD
Sometimes, for the sake of education,
discipline is required. This can come
in the form of tedious tasks or even a
quick switch on the bottom! However,
for discipline to be effective (and not a
reflection of the dispenser's pride), the
punishment must cause more sorrow to
the giver than to the receiver. Such is the
sacrifice when taking a parental role.

SECOND

THE HARMONIOUS CHILD
In this case, gentleness and compassion
will achieve the desired results. Giving
responsibility to the wife will bring forth
good tidings. If there is no wife, then
finding one will bring good fortune. When
the eldest and youngest sons balance their
power, they will be capable of taking over
the household.

THIRD

THE MOTHERLESS CHILD
The woman stares moon-eyed at gaudy
displays of wealth. Such a woman is
irresponsible and not fit to marry. For the
sake of the child, better to turn our seeking
in another direction.

FOURTH

THE DREAMY CHILD
He who only looks to the sky does
not see the viper underfoot. Pay
attention!

FIFTH

THE INNOCENT CHILD
Laughter in the fields: youthful pranks
in innocence can only bring smiles.
Tonight, he will sleep well on her bosom.

SIXTH

TREADING THE CHILD
Discipline is sometimes required, but
discipline without proper measure and
timing can sometimes create enmity
in the child and produce quite the
opposite of the desired effect. Better
to try and prevent the wrong before it
is committed than expend energy on
calculating the punishment.

ALL SIX

THE RUNAWAY CHILD
The balance in the home is forgotten.
The child runs to the north and the east.
Instead of chasing, we should focus on
remedying our own faults. After we have
resolved ourselves, the child will return
of his own accord.

*"Rain cannot be forced,
but will come at the appointed hour.
It furthers our purpose to cross
the great water."*

5

CLOUDS

WAITING

Clouds Rising to Heaven

The wise man understands that the most important
action is sometimes non-action. This is now the case as
we wait patiently on our perch and watch as the white
clouds rise from the valley to the zenith of Heaven.
There may be danger present, and through the action
of calculated inaction we will wait until this passes and
thus win the confidence of others. It may also be time
to begin planning a journey or a period of relaxation.

FIRST

CLOUDS ON THE OUTSKIRTS

We stay away from the limelight by setting up camp on the outskirts of town and focusing on ordinary affairs. We do nothing extravagant, but rather rest our bones until called back to action.

SECOND

CLOUDS ON THE BEACH

We sit by the water and observe events without getting our feet wet. This apparent inactivity may give rise to harmless gossip among those with too much time on their hands. The wise man will eventually prosper thanks to patient observation.

THIRD

CLOUDS ON THE MUD

We have taken too much upon our shoulders and are now stuck in the mud as danger encircles us. If we remain steadfast and trudge forward, placing one foot in front of the other, then we shall remain free from harm.

FOURTH

CLOUDS OF BLOOD

There is slaughter on all sides. Brother turns against brother and father against son. We should not participate in the deeds of blood, but rather preserve our power by carefully observing the slaughter and making plans to rebuild.

FIFTH

CLOUDS ON FEASTDAY

Nothing is to be accomplished today.
Better to drink red wine and dance with
a lover. Tomorrow is another day.

SIXTH

CLOUDS ON THE TOWER

It is difficult to see far. Better to the
descend into the earth and look inward.
Three mysterious guests will arrive
without invitation. It would be wise to
treat them with honor and receive them
as old friends. They will speak pertinent
wisdom without being aware that they
are giving counsel.

ALL SIX

DRAGONS IN THE CLOUDS

War! The clouds burst asunder and an
army of fierce dragons pours forth to
do battle on the plains. We are in the
midst of war. There is no retreat, no
negotiation and no surrender. No quarter
will be given. We must fight for our life.
Good luck!

"Conflict, though unavoidable, shall not be drawn to completion. Do not travel. Heed wisdom from those who have come before."

6

CLAWS

FIRST BLOOD

Sky and Water in Opposition

Dogs will bark while the tiger hunches and bares its claws. The crowd falls silent to observe the ensuing conflict. Attempting the middle passage will bring some success, yet to pursue relentlessly will surely lead to disaster. It is advised to take counsel from a wise elder nearby and not to travel; for this would surely lead to a watery grave.

訟 CLAWS

CLIPPING THE CLAWS

Sometimes karma may only be resolved by carrying the conflict to the finish; while at other times it is better to hold our tongue and let things pass. This is one of those times when it is advised to shift our focus away from the conflict and let the tension fade away with the passage of time. By doing so, we accord with the balance of Heaven and Earth. Say nothing!

RETRACTING THE CLAWS

The wise man knows when he is overwhelmed. To continue to fight will lead to our ultimate demise. Better to place pride in our pocket, gathering our most loyal followers and making a hasty retreat to the mountains. We shall live to fight another day.

SHARPENING THE CLAWS

Cultivating our own power may lead to jealousy in others. They may try to attack, but their power is uncultivated and easily put down. That said, it is still not advisable to step into the public sphere, for there still is much work to be done on the home front.

FOURTH

COVERING THE CLAWS
The conflict cannot be resolved through further warfare. An offer of peace must be made and accepted if there is to be hope for either party.

FIFTH

BARRING THE CLAWS
The desert wind rests on our left shoulder. We should attack immediately and without remorse. Our cause is mandated by Heaven and victory is assured by the hand that writes the future as if it were the past.

SIXTH

RESPECTING THE CLAWS
The wise warrior buries his fallen enemy with armor and sword intact. That is to say that prizes won in battle should be left with the deceased. To wear a dead man's crown will only bring misfortune.

ALL SIX

CLEANING THE CLAWS
There is a time for action and a time for no action. Better now to take a solitary walk to the river and wash our claws in the sand. It is strongly advised to rest or take a relaxing journey.

"Gathering mass inward,
the sage chains the tiger,
and prepares for deployment."

THE ARMY

ATTACK

Land Overtaking Water

Whether we think ourselves as businessman, warrior or monk, all life is a battle and should be treated as such. The army executes the will of its king. Soldiers are drawn from surrounding villages for honor and discipline to be bestowed upon them. Recruit those without purpose and train them in the skills necessary to execute your will.

師 THE ARMY

FIRST

TRAINING THE ARMY
The wise general teaches the army how to
march properly. If a man is capable of doing
one thing perfectly, he is capable of doing
all things perfectly. A soldier following
an order without hesitation may be the
difference between victory and death.
Without discipline, disaster will strike.

SECOND

THE GENERAL'S ARMY
The army is only as effective as its general,
who is only as effective as his king. The
wise man would honor his general three
times and place faith in him to follow
orders properly and at his own discretion.

THIRD

CAUSALITIES OF THE ARMY
The ravens circle; the wagons are laden
with corpses. Our enemy attacked us
while we were sleeping. Be on guard
for that which is unseen.

FOURTH

THE ARMY RETREATS
Military campaigns are concerned with
one thing only: Victory. That said, only
a fool would advance when the wise man
would halt and retreat. Battle should be
fought on another day when the odds are
more favorable.

FIFTH

THE ARMY UNDER SIEGE
Rabid wolves roam the countryside as
the army sets camp and posts sentries.
The wise man keeps his thoughts to
himself and does not discuss plans with
subordinates. The oldest son should be
placed in command, while the younger
son is a lout and not suitable for any role
save carrying the corpses. We should hold
our ground.

SIXTH

THE PRINCE'S ARMY
He rides forth on a gallant steed.
Command should be given to a kind man
whose words inspire sincerity and respect.
To allow a man of harsh words to take
the reins will surely lead to disaster.

ALL SIX

THE ARMY DISBANDS
The rebels have been quelled and have
now joined the alliance. There is no
longer any need to retain so many soldiers.
We should send our men home to their
families and maintain a small honor
guard to remind the populace what
we are capable of.

*"Sitting first in a circle of equals,
we should consult with the alliance,
for this shall bring correct merit."*

THE COVEN

ALLIANCE

Water upon the Land

The coven is a circle for those with troubled hearts.
Leaning upon each other for support allows the many
to complete that which was impossible for the one.
We should treat our neighbors as we would like to be
treated ourselves and consult the oracle once again
for counsel from the coven.

FIRST

THE COVEN OF CONFIDENCE
The support of our peers allows us the
confidence to face insurmountable odds
and emerge victorious. Good fortune
will arise from unexpected places. The
wind is coming.

SECOND

THE INNER COVEN
The family sits down for a meal; the
father presides. We become closer to
those already close to us. We trust in
their support, since strength received
from the coven leads us to success.

THIRD

THE TWISTED COVEN
He opens his eyes and realizes that the
coven is black: a place from which fear
and delusion will spew forth. Some
difficult choices must be made.

FOURTH

OUTSIDE THE COVEN
Melodious music is heard on the other
side of town. The wise man steps outside
his immediate circle to seek further
assistance.

FIFTH

THE EXCLUSIVE COVEN
The game slips away: not enough hands
were present. By excluding those who
wish to join our immediate circle, we
bring about difficulty for ourselves. Better
to be open and accepting to all, for their
assistance may soon be required in the
most unexpected way.

SIXTH

THE HEADLESS COVEN
He is lost in the forest, so he retraces his
steps and then calls for help. A group
without a leader is not a group. The
leader brings different minds together
and performs the necessary tasks of
administration. Attempts to move forward
without this unifying and practical
presence will surely lead to disaster.

ALL SIX

THE COVEN TRANSFORMS
Through the guidance of a wise leader,
the coven evolves from a circle to a
triangle. Within a triangle, the leadership
role is definite as we begin to focus on
more concrete and practical tasks.

"*Clouds gather, yet rain will not fall.
The whip may crack, yet the horse
walks, not runs.*"

THE KETTLE

SWELLING

Wind across the Heavens

The kettle sits on the stove, but the water will not boil. Clouds come from the west, but the land remains like a desert; we must drink the tea lukewarm. We will find success in accomplishing smaller things; as for serious matters, it is advised to wait until another day to move forward.

小畜 THE KETTLE

FIRST

PURCHASING THE KETTLE
Scouring the pawnshops, he finds that
which he seeks. She sits alone on a dusty
shelf and shines with a radiance visible
only to his eye. There is praise only for
those who stand behind what they love.

SECOND

REFURBISHING THE KETTLE
He returns to the place of his birth to
ask assistance for the proper method
of polishing the silver. We may wish to
stop and look over our shoulder, and
even consider turning back as there
may be some valuable information
we have missed.

THIRD

THE BROKEN KETTLE
The handle separates from the body,
it clanks to the floor; husband and wife
place the blame upon each other and glare
cross-eyed. Why must it be like this?

FOURTH

FILLING THE KETTLE
Following instructions carefully, he fills
the kettle with the correct mixture. Our
elders stand in confidence behind us.
By following tried and true methods,
we will avoid spilling the water.

FIFTH

PLACING THE KETTLE
We lower it confidently onto the flame.
We invite our neighbors over for tea so
as to win their hearts. The wise man's
wealth is in his generosity.

SIXTH

THE KETTLE SINGS
The clouds burst asunder and the
nourishing rains fall. People should gather
close and share a warm cup of tea. Women
are advised to refrain from persistence,
while men are advised to wait until the
full moon to take action.

ALL SIX

THE KETTLE EXPLODES
Unbounded passion rules for but a
moment. Experience it, grow from
it and then let it go.

"*The weak treads upon the strong.*
With doubt comes failure."

10

THE RAZOR

TREADING

Water Open to the Sky

We walk through the valley of darkness, yet we fear no evil. He treads upon the tail of the tiger, but he is not bitten. Balancing upon the razor's edge, we move forward slowly and with confidence. Provided that we do not look back or doubt our actions, we will find success in that which we undertake. Fear is the mind-killer. Do not fear.

履   THE RAZOR

FIRST

REDUCING THE RAZOR
Reducing the problem to its most basic
element is the path of the wise man.
Leaving his companions and baggage
behind, the hunter stalks into the
forest with loincloth and bow. Divide
and conquer.

SECOND

CONCEALING THE RAZOR
The wise man looks within for answers,
and finds wisdom in the peaceful solution.
The hunter lays down his bow and retreats
to the mountain, following the middle
path. If there is confusion, perhaps now
is the time for peaceful contemplation.

THIRD

THE UNSEEN RAZOR
His left eye is injured, he thinks to move
forward, but is unable to see the crouching
tiger upon the road. We should only
proceed at the request of a strong and
wise elder; for they will be able to perceive
things to which we are blind. To do
otherwise may lead to permanent injury.

FOURTH

THE RAZOR'S EDGE
Removing his shoes, the hunter quietly stalks into the cave of the tiger. Fear is nothing more than an influx of power. Harness this power and confront the adversary with confidence. Success is presaged for those who hold their breath and proceed with confidence.

FIFTH

AVOIDING THE RAZOR
The razor is too sharp and the encroaching winds make balance impossible. Better to bow our head and find another way.

SIXTH

OMENS OF THE RAZOR
The flight of a raven leads the hunter to a watering hole. Look to the sky for an omen and proceed with the confidence of righteous action.

ALL SIX

THE RAZOR BREAKS
The bowstring snaps, the hunter chips his knife. Perhaps today is not the day for action.

"As above, so below.
Those in the heavens embrace
the terrestrial,
while those on the earth pay
tribute to the sky."

11

THE MIRROR

PERFECTION

Heaven and Earth in Harmony

By seeing ourselves as simply a reflection of the people
and places all around us, we are able to achieve peace
in our environment. This is presaged because we
understand that all people are truly the same, with the
same joys, fears, goals, wishes and desires as ourselves.
We shall find peace in our own heart and watch it
reflected in the world that surrounds us.

FIRST

BEHIND THE MIRROR

Pulling up the weeds in his master's garden, the gardener finds a golden coin buried deep within the earth. We should proceed according to plan and fix our mind upon the notion of "leading through following". If we do this, then we will find what we seek as well as an unexpected bonus.

SECOND

THE UNBREAKABLE MIRROR

Wildflowers flourish in the desert sands. No need to wait for a boat, he can walk on water. The mountain may seem far away, but he does not retreat and takes care not to abandon his companions. We currently possess great power. As long as we focus on constant forward motion, all that is asked will come to fruition. Do not retreat. All is well.

THIRD

THE ECLIPSED MIRROR

The sun may be momentarily black, but this too will pass. Every going forth is followed by a return, and in the end we shall still be alive, and stronger from the experience. Continue forward with persistence and faith. The darkest hour of the night is the hour that precedes dawn.

FOURTH

POLISHING THE MIRROR
As the tides of creation dictate, sometimes we must lead and sometimes follow. This is the time to bow our heads and serve others by polishing their mirror. We gain nothing directly for ourselves, and even if others should seem ungrateful, we will continue to serve with diligence and trust in our hearts.

FIFTH

THE VANITY MIRROR
The king's daughter primps herself and prepares for marriage to one of her father's closest allies. It would be best now to be impartial and make decisions based on need and logic, forgoing emotional attachments.

SIXTH

THE MIRROR SHATTERS
Calamity strikes, the castle wall is breached. We should not fight this exterior force, but rather focus on maintaining order among our own people. Although we have done our best, we will still be blamed.

ALL SIX

THE OTHER SIDE OF THE MIRROR
If we gaze into the Abyss long enough, the Abyss will start to gaze back at us. Prepare for a dark time.

"All is broken.
Refusing payment and a silent
retreat are the only hope of
averting disaster."

THE BARGAIN

BLOCKAGES

Heaven and Earth in Opposition

Those who are vicious and dishonorable in speech and conduct will now flourish as the righteous man is put into chains and thrown into the dungeon. Momentary success can be found through unbridled fear and anger. Sadly, the man who wishes not to take this polluted route must humbly bow his head and bite his lip as the land is destroyed around him. Choose carefully, do what you will, but be prepared to pay the price when the contract is completed.

否　THE BARGAIN

FIRST

BONUS TO THE BARGAIN
Serving his master accordingly; scouring
the land, the supplicant discovers
an unexpected golden coin amid the
debris. Following this path, we will
find unexpected good fortune.

SECOND

SEALING THE BARGAIN
A drop of blood in the inkwell sets the
supplicant upon a long dark road. The
unpolluted man now retreats from the
populace to avoid becoming entangled
with their daily business.

THIRD

CONCEALING THE BARGAIN
There is much shame and regret regarding
past affairs. To remedy the situation,
action is favored over words.

FOURTH

SERVING THE BARGAIN
He who follows his master's command
cannot be blamed. He blends in with the
crowd and walks with equally obedient
companions. We should now do what
we are told, as the force that commands
is stronger than we are and cannot be
reckoned with.

FIFTH

FINISHING THE BARGAIN
That which was agreed is almost
completed, and we are a few steps from
regaining our freedom. But we must also
be aware that this is when the danger is at
its greatest. That said, we must bind our
possessions closely and remain diligent.

SIXTH

THE BARGAIN COMPLETED
That which has been borrowed is now
returned as all parties face each other
again on equal footing. It is finished,
let all pass, and go forth, young soldier!

ALL SIX

THE BARGAIN RECONSIDERED
Perhaps all was not as it seemed? Perhaps
we were fooled by a mask of illusion?
Perhaps this dark path was not necessary?
Perhaps success can be found through
honorable word and action? Perhaps.

"Arriving as two, departing as one. With correct understanding of roles, there shall be fruition."

13

THE BELOVED

MATING

The Sun and Fire as Lovers

The young prince narrows his sight. All he can see is the radiant beauty of his lonesome bride as the monk submits to the will of the Creator. The power a woman gains over a man in the unfolding of love may be a necessary step in the cycle of creation. The wise man continues what he has started and contemplates a journey.

FIRST

THE BELOVED AT THE DOOR
He sits alone by the fire, as the blizzard
rages outside. There is a knock. He
opens the door to find his beloved asking
for entrance. To refuse this would be
unspeakable.

SECOND

THE BELOVED IS RELATED
He discovers his beloved is a distant
cousin: possible unforeseen trouble.
Whether by blood or social ties, it is now
advised not to join with one who has been
raised in the same clan. This will squelch
the power of the man, for she will forever
see him through the eyes of his mother.

THIRD

COWERING FROM THE BELOVED
Why is it that a man will seek something
so diligently, but when the time has come
to make the decisive move, he cowers
and retreats to the hills? Such cowardice
deserves three years of misery. Boldness
is required.

FOURTH

THE BELOVED IS FORTIFIED
The defenses are too strong, he is unable
to breach the castle wall. He will lay siege
to the gate and fend off any potential
invaders. Entry will not be gained via
force, but rather through a request for

fresh supplies. The wise man maintains a sense of what is right when encountering difficult situations. Be stubborn, yet forever kind.

FIFTH

THE BELOVED IN THE CROWD
Cooped up in the house, they can find only arguments and weeping. They separate and disperse independently into the crowd. Here the joyous song and dance of the community reminds them of their love and brings them together as an extension of the clan.

SIXTH

SEPARATED FROM THE BELOVED
He is sent away to distant lands while she tends the fire and weeps. This is not what we have expected. We should not regret this situation, for it is deemed necessary by the tides of creation. Take the time to examine if this goal is really worth sacrificing everything to attain.

ALL SIX

UNION WITH THE BELOVED
After a painstaking journey, the river finally meets the sea. We will attain what we seek, for we awake and realize that it was she who has been seeking us all along.

*"Compassion while sitting
in the seat of power shall be
rewarded with great possession."*

TREASURE!

DRAGON'S GOLD

Fire in the Heavens

大有

The dragon sits upon a horde of gold. The wise man
has access to the resources to enact and bear fruits
of the will. All that can be won by physical means
will be so acquired, but remember that there are
some things that have no price and must be
attained by merit.

大有 TREASURE!

FIRST

FAULTLESS TREASURE

The taxes are paid and the contracts have been fulfilled. Whatever treasure we hold should be considered ours, clean and clear. If attempts are made to draw us again into the soiled deeds of others, then it is advised to remain blameless and unnoticed.

SECOND

SPENDING THE TREASURE

Our deposits are healthy and well protected from danger. If there is an undertaking that will require the expenditure of resources, then it is advised to move forward at this time.

THIRD

THE DISTINGUISHED TREASURE

The sword remains lodged in the stone. Scores of ordinary men attempt to claim the honor of extracting this treasure, but only the true king succeeds. That is to say: unless we are masters of our domain and stand well above our peers, then it is advised not to attempt this goal.

FOURTH

HUMBLE BEFORE THE TREASURE

He recognizes that his vast supply of wealth lies within his possession through no merit of his own. That said, he bows humbly and is thankful for what he has been given to steward.

FIFTH

DONNING THE TREASURE

She wears a fine silk dress while mingling with the crowd. Our high social standing and acquired merit allow us to act regally and unexpectedly when dealing with the common people.

SIXTH

BLESSINGS OF THE TREASURE

The hand that writes the future as if it were the past guides our actions, offering us protection and assured success as we step confidently toward our goals. Good times are ahead.

ALL SIX

DISPERSING THE TREASURE

The prince stands on the podium and throws coins to the peasants. They now sing his praises. In some forms, perhaps money *can* buy love?

*"Reduce that which is full
while supplementing
that which is lacking."*

THE MONK

MODESTY

A Mountain in the Earth

The first shall be last and the last shall be first. The wise man knows there is a time to shine and a time to whisper. Now is the occasion to practice modesty, to walk very lightly and to leave no trace. The public dislikes that which is full and reveres that which is empty. Working from the small hours of the night through to the glow of the dawn, the monk takes from where there is too much to augment that which has too little.

謙 THE MONK

FIRST

THE WANDERING MONK
Leaving the confines of the monastery,
the monk returns to the world to practice
acts of humility. If there is no boat to
take him across the river, he will simply
walk on water. We shall now go forth
on a journey and let nothing stop us.

SECOND
/

THE HEART OF THE MONK
To the ear, the morning call of the cock is
scarcely audible. However, to the heart of
the monk, the heralding of the new golden
dawn rings true. Following the whispers
of our heart, we go forth with confidence.

THIRD

THE WORKING MONK
Leading through example and not by
command, the wise man throws his
energies into the details of his work.
He barely notices the people all around
him. They come to admire his ironclad
work ethic and submit to his will.

FOURTH

THE GARDENER MONK
Planting seeds in the fall will result in
new growth in the spring. We should
walk lightly and begin to plan and
cultivate that which we wish to achieve.

FIFTH

THE SOCIABLE MONK
He invites his neighbors over for tea and serves them from wooden cups. It is best now to be hospitable and not display our wealth, so as to lull those who would oppose us into a false sense of security. If there are rebels, it would be best to crush them now.

SIXTH

THE WARRIOR MONK
The staff is just as useful for fighting as it is for walking. It would be best now to take a stance of righteous aggression, to correct what has been wronged and to subdue those who will not submit to the Word from above.

ALL SIX

THE MONK RENOUNCES
Overwhelmed by circumstances, the monk removes his robes and dons the clothing of the common man. We have done all that we can by working with the mind and the spirit. Now is the time to get our hands dirty and to work with the flesh and the blood.

*"Drawing strength
from four directions,
shockwaves resonate to the core."*

THE HAMMER

FEROCITY

Thunder on the Earth

The hammer strikes the anvil, causing sparks to
fly and shaping that which was previously thought
unshapeable. The funeral dirge hums as the wise man
gathers his resources and prepares to set forth to enact
his will. Anything that is solid will be shaped under the
pressure of the hammer. But be aware that upon things
such as water (the feminine) and wind (the formless)
the hammer will have no effect.

FIRST

THE WEIGHTY HAMMER
The cock is sleepy, his call does not rouse
men from their slumber. The hammer
is too heavy and the arm fails under its
weight. Perhaps we have taken upon
ourselves a load too great for our strength
and have failed on account of exhaustion.

SECOND

THE HAMMER STRIKES TRUE
Following the plans he has previously
laid out, the wise man strikes with
confidence. Be like a rock. Consistency
leads to success.

THIRD

THE HAMMER IS LATE
Too much time spent in contemplation
and fear has caused us to miss the
opportunity. Regret may surface owing
to this blundering irresponsibility.
Courage is required.

FOURTH

BRANDING THE HAMMER
Making alliance with the government
inspector, the hammer is approved and
validated as an enforcer of will. We have
the support of official bodies behind our
action, which will soon come to fruition.

FIFTH

THE CHIPPED HAMMER

A foreign object was hidden in the anvil: the hammer is chipped. This can be likened to the coming of a slight illness. Fear not, for the illness is acute and will soon pass.

SIXTH

HURRYING THE HAMMER

We have almost waited too long before taking action. But be aware that we still have a final chance and that if we hurry and act with extreme rashness, then we will still have the opportunity for success.

ALL SIX

THE HAMMER BREAKS

Too much, too fast has exhausted the stock of our merit. There is nothing more we can do except make preparations for the next turn of the wheel.

*"To lead is to follow.
From consideration arises respect."*

THE LEADER

FOLLOWING

Thunder in the Lake

A leader is one who has the trust of his followers and executes directives as a function of the people. Leaders will come in different forms at different times. The king sits at the top of a pyramid, issuing ultimatums; while the chief sits at the start and end point of a circle, and is regarded as a first among equals. Now is the time to seek out the confident leader either within or without, and follow his command to victory.

FIRST

SEEKING THE LEADER
There is a change of heart among those in command. They consider previously discarded alternatives. The wise man leaves the comforts of his home to venture into the marketplace to purchase produce and listen for whispers in the crowd.

SECOND

REJECTING THE LEADER
He refuses responsibility and prefers to run in the forest with his childhood friends. Rejecting the adult and serving the child is a joyful way to live, but does not get much done that is useful.

THIRD

SERVING THE LEADER
He rejects his childhood playmates and pledges fealty to the king. By doing so, he strengthens his position and patiently waits for command before taking action.

FOURTH

THE CORRUPTED LEADER
He opens his eyes and realizes that the leader is polluted and only interested in serving his own secret motives. In this situation, the wise man will continue service to the corrupted leader by focusing on being a beacon of sincerity and working in the shadows to right wrongs and lay seeds for the impending coup.

FIFTH

FOLLOWING THE LEADER
The young knight places his utmost
trust in his king as he is led blindly into
the forest. By having faith in those who
lead us, we shall find success.

SIXTH

A NEW LEADER IS CROWNED
After spending time in seclusion on the
Western Mountain, the prince returns
to find himself hailed as the new king.
The old king had exhausted his merit
and was deemed no longer fit to rule.
Learn from the past and do not repeat
the same mistakes.

ALL SIX

THE LEADER IS ASSASSINATED!
Bandits roam the countryside; the queen
is in conspiracy and a subtle poison is
slipped into the wine. Do we still drink?

"Corruption repeats itself unless experiences are re-lived and thus corrected."

THE GHOST

DECAY

Wind at the Foot of the Mountain

As the corpse is lowered into the earth, a disembodied spirit rises forth. What happened once will surely happen again as the ghost repeats the experiences of its physical life in the attempt to understand and in order to resolve the countless cycles of death and rebirth. The wise man knows that this is a good time to break from routine and possibly take an inner or outer voyage of renewal.

蠱 THE GHOST

FIRST

SACRIFICING TO THE GHOST
The child takes charge of the family
holdings and places three sticks of incense
upon his father's grave. The wise man
takes responsibility for the mistakes
of those-who-have-come-before and
rectifies the trouble as his own.

SECOND

THE MOTHER'S GHOST
Placing flowers on his mother's grave,
the wise man seeks to complete that which
was left undone. This responsibility is
small, yet necessary. A calm, balanced
approach should be taken.

THIRD

THE FATHER'S GHOST
Placing a golden coin upon his father's
grave, the wise man forgoes his own
responsibilities. Have no regret when
expending resources to balance past
affairs. In the end, all will be attained
and all shall be free of blame.

FOURTH

FIGHTING THE GHOST
The boy does nothing as the angry ghost
indiscriminately destroys the home. There
is a time for sacrifice, a time for tolerance
and a time for enmity. Stand up now against
destructive spirits and exorcise them
without remorse, as a priest would a devil.

FIFTH

EMBRACING THE GHOST

Following the direction of his father's ghost, the boy comes upon a healing spring and the people bestow honors upon him. The wise man does not fight the whispers in his head, but rather understands that All is One and accepts what is offered. It may be more than expected.

SIXTH

MERGING WITH THE GHOST

Taking all into himself, the wise man realizes that he is alone and stands on top of a pyramid. As long as action is taken without hesitation or stopping to take counsel from others, our will can now usurp even the king.

ALL SIX

FREEING THE GHOST

Through a heartfelt sacrifice and correct action, the ghost is freed from its ceaseless wandering and allowed a final rest. All deals are finished, delivered and paid for. This is the end of one cycle and the beginning of another. We are free to advance in any direction we may choose, as all now are equal. Choose wisely!

*"As we settle to work on affairs,
the path is clear yet we must
keep our eyes open."*

THE PATH

APPROACH

Land above a Lake

The companions approach the base of the mountain as the path winding upward becomes visible. We should move forward with a slow, steady confidence, but be aware that further up the mountain, the path fails and we will be forced to blaze a trail. That is to say, the first leg will be easy, but further along in the future, we can expect significant difficulties.

臨 THE PATH

FIRST

A WELL-WORN PATH
The road we chose is popular and true,
being tested and worn by countless
generations. Now is the time not to rebel,
but rather to move forward, following the
advice of those who have come before.

SECOND

A STRAGGLER ON THE PATH
The companions set forth on the tried
path, while one breaks from the group to
find an alternative route. He will surely
become lost in the forest. The leader
should rebuke him and then let the
matter be forgotten, for there are
greater struggles ahead.

THIRD

A USELESS PATH
The bags are packed and the companions
are ready to set forth. Alas, the leader
receives a message by carrier pigeon
that it would not be advantageous to
move forward at this time. Best to let it
pass and wait for another opportunity.

FOURTH

THE SHINING PATH
The road is well marked, the sky is blue
and the mountain beckons us onward.
All the omens are in accord. Move
forward with confidence while taking
care to avoid unnecessary mistakes.

FIFTH

THE MIDDLE PATH

The wise man studies the omens and carefully contemplates before moving forward. He balances left against right, gain against loss, before taking the intelligent approach of the middle path.

SIXTH

THE SECRET PATH

Waking before dawn, the wise man scurries into the forest alone and discovers a secret path up the mountain; he tells no one. It would be best now to not discuss our will or goals with others, but rather silently move forward and wait for them at the top of the mountain.

ALL SIX

ERASING THE PATH

We have successfully reached our goal and have stored enough provisions to keep our strength up, as well as that of our companions. Better now to cover our tracks, erasing the path, for if more come, then all shall go hungry.

*"To see and be seen,
yet not make contact."*

THE TOWER

OBSERVATION

Wind across the Earth

The tower is a place for contemplation, preparation and observation. The wise man ascends the steps to distance himself from other people and gain perspective on the cycles of joy and pain in himself, in the populace and in the seasons. Though it will sometimes be necessary to ascend the tower, keep in mind that standing on the tower is only a preparation for action. It can be considered the first step along a seven-step road. The sacrifice of blood, sweat and tears must still be performed.

觀 THE TOWER

FIRST

THE TOY TOWER
It is acceptable for a child to play at being an adult, but a man with responsibilities pretending to be child? What is this? Priorities need to be realigned and responsibility taken.

SECOND

THE SPY TOWER
Although it may seem slightly embarrassing, the wise man gains advantage at this time by setting spies to keep secret watch at the door cracks and listen for whispers in the wind. The information gained in this way may prove invaluable.

THIRD

THE STRATEGY TOWER
Ascending the steps, the wise man takes personal time to find silence. From this silence, he will gain perspective of his situation and make the confident decision whether to advance or retreat.

FOURTH

INSPECTING THE TOWER
Before committing to action, the wise man may wish to wander from realm to realm, inspecting and carefully weighing the pros and cons of each option before coming to a final decision.

FIFTH

THE WATCH TOWER

With concern for their well-being, the wise man climbs the tower to keep watch upon the people that surround him. He does this because he may be able to perceive things that others cannot.

SIXTH

THE CONTEMPLATION TOWER

There is a correct moment for everything, and now is the time to separate ourselves from the lives of other people and take the opportunity to understand and rectify our own troubles.

ALL SIX

DESCENDING THE TOWER

The time for observation and contemplation is now finished as we take counsel from a wise one and make plans to direct our intentions toward the south and the west.

*"Removing the obstruction
by employing details of
past encounters."*

21

THE LAW

GNAWING

Lightning and Thunder

噬嗑

The wise ones who have come before authored the code of the law to bring Order to where there was Chaos. The intention is to set all persons upon equal footing so they can be judged without bias. Of course, one must also consider the natural order of things and whether the law being enforced is the original intention of justice or the prostitution of some clever trickster. Now is the time to analyze our affairs to a hair, leaving no stone unturned and considering every last detail for its potential advantage. We must gnaw the meat to the bone and make soup from what is left. At this juncture, the wise man calls in all debts and uses even the subtlest point to make his case.

噬嗑 THE LAW

FIRST

THE LAW ENFORCED
Those who are dishonorable in speech
and action should have their ankles
shackled, so as to not cause any more
trouble. We should be firm, enforce our
punishment and then turn our attention
to other affairs.

SECOND

LOST IN THE LAW
He becomes so engrossed in the details
of the work that he fails to see the greater
picture. Such negligence makes a difficult
time for all.

THIRD

THE POISONED LAW
As he stays up all night, studying the texts,
a spider creeps up and bites him. This
indicates an adversary using the details of
the law to bring us harm. Fear not: accept
treatment and the poison will prove acute.

FOURTH

THE IRON LAW
Beating his head against a wall, he achieves
nothing but a bloody scalp. There will be
sunshine on the other side, but perhaps
now a different approach is merited.

FIFTH

THE GOLDEN LAW
Scouring the texts, he discovers a golden
coin embedded within the pages: this is
all he will find. Accept the good fortune
bestowed and do not press the matter.

SIXTH

DEAF TO THE LAW
Wearing earmuffs protects us from the
cold, but at the same time obstructs our
hearing. Best now to not put any trust
in our own judgment, for we are
temporarily muddled.

ALL SIX

BREAKING THE LAW
Every dam must have its release valve as
the wise man now goes against convention
and does what must be done to let the
water flow. Do not get caught!

*"Inner beauty whispers and
subdues current affairs.
Those of controversy wait
for another day."*

22

THE
CELEBRATION

ELEGANCE

Fire at the Foot of the Mountain

People come together in elegance and beauty. This is the
time for drink, song and dance. One should take one's lover
forcefully by the hand and spin around the dance floor. For
the wise man, now is the time to renew acquaintances, plot
alliances and reconcile enemies in this informal meeting
place. The celebration is not the meat – only the bones.
It is a staging ground for the future. That said, only small
things should be undertaken. During the celebration, one
should always remain upright and guarded in speech.
For things said in jest can have large repercussions
in the world.

FIRST

WALKING TO THE CELEBRATION

Adorned in his finest garments, he refuses a ride and walks alone to savor the fresh evening breeze. The wise man stands strong and alone and does not accept unneeded help, for he knows that everything has its price.

SECOND

CONFORMING FOR THE CELEBRATION

Perusing the finest shops, the wise man chooses a suit of contemporary and conservative cut. On the inside, we should be what we are; but on the outside, it is best now to conform to social norms. Have nothing to prove. Every advantage counts!

THIRD

THE CELEBRATION BEGINS

The doors swing wide and the prince steps forth, shining down to the laces of his boots. If we stand strong and bright in the image we project, then no one can stop us from achieving our goal.

FOURTH

SUSPICION AT THE CELEBRATION

He has donned a fresh white suit, but his arrival is delayed by having to attend to the affairs of a maiden. There is suspicion in the air about the motives of a certain person, but upon further examination, we find that this person serves an honorable intention.

FIFTH

UNDERDRESSED FOR THE CELEBRATION

While everybody else is wearing their finest silks, he shows up in the clothing of the common man. Fear not, he will find good fortune even if he does not deserve it.

SIXTH

A SIMPLE CELEBRATION

Drinking from wooden cups, the young ones gather round as the wise man weaves the tale of his life. We are master of this situation; what we desire we will attain through simple forward motion.

ALL SIX

EXITING THE CELEBRATION

Packing his bags, he concedes that all that could be done has been done. That said, he leaves this cycle behind and sets off in search of new adventure.

"Hold to nothing,
allow the remainder to fade.
Give gracefully to those below."

LAUNDRY

SHEDDING

Mountain upon the Earth

Sometimes our clothes get dirty and we must take time off from the world to deal with this inward concern. We have been soiled on all sides and a destructive force has managed to gain power over us. It is useless to fight this force as all our cards have already been displayed. Now is the time to cut our losses and go into retreat to allow this negative energy to be washed away like a stain upon our shirt. This also implies standing complete and alone; and letting those ties fade away that we may have for certain people or places.

剥 LAUNDRY

FIRST

SORTING THE LAUNDRY
He separates the light from the dark,
recognizing each from an unbiased
viewpoint. Those under our care display
no consistency in their action. Best to be
done with them and focus on other things.

SECOND

THE NEIGHBOR'S LAUNDRY
These are not my pants! The wise man
recognizes and is able to differentiate
between his own problems and those
that another attempts to project onto
him. He now politely ignores them with an
iron will, even if previously he had called
them "friend". We should not take this
lightly: we must stand firm or we will
be destroyed.

THIRD

BLEACHING THE LAUNDRY
He uses the whole bottle, no color will
remain! The wise man inwardly isolates
himself and severs relations with those who
stand above and those who stand below.
It is only in this way that we may be free!

FOURTH

AN INTRUDER IN THE LAUNDRY
A red sock mixed in with the whites?
Everything will be pink! It is an utter
disaster. How could we have avoided this?

FIFTH

FOLDING THE LAUNDRY
The handmaiden folds the fresh clothes,
imbuing them with her jasmine scent. This
outward matter being taken care of, we are
free to move forward without regret.

SIXTH

THE LAUNDRY IS WRINKLED
He does not accept help when it is offered.
The man who is unkind in word and
action will be stripped of his own home.
However, the kind man will be offered
passage to new and exotic lands.

ALL SIX

HANDWASHING THE LAUNDRY
Disregarding modern machinery, we
take the high and lonely road to achieve
our goal. Working in the shadows, the
wise man remains diligent and focuses
on details of the process.

"On the seventh day comes return.
Only upon arrival shall rest
be taken."

THE RETURN

TURNING

Thunder in the Earth

What has been borrowed will be restored, he who has gone forth will return henceforth. The entire cycle of creation occurs in seven days, with return on the sixth and rest on the seventh. The return is a time to seek out our roots, the place where we began, and to gather strength from this source. It is best to firmly choose this concrete thing to return to, and charge like a bull, without even taking the time to smell the flowers along the road.

復 THE RETURN

FIRST

RETURNING FROM THE CROSSROADS
The day is late and he stands alone upon the dusty road. The omens presage turning back before we have gone too far. Better to have a warm bed and meal tonight. Nothing will be lost by this.

SECOND

A BLESSED RETURN
The hand that writes the future as if it were the past dictates our return at this juncture. We shall find extreme good fortune by following this path. This is also the time to bestow compassion upon those less fortunate.

THIRD

MANY RETURNS
Every time he puts a foot outside, he is forced to turn back owing to conditions within or without. There is too much happening to cleave a clean path through the forest. If we persist, then we will be turned back continually and end up wasting our power.

FOURTH

A SOLITARY RETURN
His companions are sluggards and drunkards, and only seek to foster indulgence and negligence. Better to leave them now and return alone.

To push forward would mean being
led to disaster owing to another
person's ineptitude.

FIFTH

RETURN OF THE KING

The exiled king is heralded by the
populace and called forth to rule the
land once again. He must return for the
higher purpose of serving the people.
But then again, he was beginning to enjoy
the solitary life.

SIXTH

A WOUNDED RETURN

Nothing is positive. The snake bites the
eagle, which drops in mid-flight. Armies
are tasked to fight, but the defeat is
total and disaster overtakes him and his
companions for ten years. Only unbiased
justice and wisdom may prevent this.

ALL SIX

A GLORIOUS RETURN

Rich with victory, he gathers his
companions and they return in glory,
laden with the spoils of battle. Let the
shops close and the people feast for two
days and three nights.

"*Remembering the original face,
those of innocent virtue shall
receive abundance.*"

THE
SURPRISE!

UNEXPECTED

A Shout from the Heavens

乞妄

The farmer sits on his hands as the rain falls
and nourishes the crops. It is time to expect the
unexpected. There is no reason to go anywhere or do
anything: we should simply do as we do and watch the
world unfold before our eyes. However, we must be
sure to maintain integrity and honor, for those lacking
in these attributes will receive quite the opposite of
a nice surprise.

FIRST

THE SURPRISE COMPLETES
The farmer waters his crops and is then given the additional boon of rainfall. The wise man acts as if no help is coming, while remaining alert for an unexpected opportunity.

SECOND

WAITING FOR THE SURPRISE
It is not advised to calculate the profits before the first seed has been planted. There is much work yet to be done before we may consider reaping the rewards. Best not to wait for the sun; rather, we shall put our head down and diligently work through the night.

THIRD

A SOILED SURPRISE
The cattle are able to graze, but it is on another's land. Every positive on one front is the negative reaction on the other – such is the way of the tides of creation. The wise man is aware that his gain is another's loss and weighs his actions carefully.

FOURTH

THE SURPRISE NOT NEEDED
The crops are ready for harvest and the birds sing. He completely forgot about the surprise that never came and instead ploughed diligently toward his goal. In the end, he achieved his desire thorough good old-fashioned sweat and blood.

FIFTH

AN INJURIOUS SURPRISE
He reaches his hand blindly under the sink and is surprised by the bite of a venomous spider. He should have looked first! For treatment, he consults traditional medical textbooks while avoiding witch doctors and faith healers.

SIXTH

NO SURPRISE
The forest is bleak and the roads are closed. Best to stay put and weather things through until the first signs of spring.

ALL SIX

THE SURPRISE EXPLODES
The cake was carrying a hidden bomb. Frosting rains for miles around as people forget themselves and engage in unbidden acts of lavishness.

*"In studying the past,
we are generous in the present."*

THE
CARRIAGE

THE GIVER

Sky amidst the Mountains

The wise man loads his carriage with valuables and food for the people while setting out on a journey across the land. By doing so, he spreads his wealth and gains the people's confidence. This is the time to leave the comforts of the home and to give freely to all we may meet upon the road. This will bring us much merit, which may be redeemed at a future date. During this time, it is also advised to avoid making enemies or passing harsh judgment.

FIRST

THE CARRIAGE STOPS

A storm looms on the mountain pass: possible trouble in the near future. The wise man does not turn back, but rather brings all activities to a temporary halt.

SECOND

THE CARRIAGE BREAKS

The axle separates from the hub. This was a long time coming and the misfortune can be blamed on the slothfulness of the mechanic. Nevertheless, it is a problem that must be dealt with in the field.

THIRD

THE HORSE'S CARRIAGE

The virile stallion pulls the carriage forward while the wise man concentrates his attention on plotting a defensive strategy to confront the encroaching storm. We must enlist others to do the mundane work while concentrating our energies on the potential adversary.

FOURTH

THE BULL'S CARRIAGE

The strength of a bull is necessary to tackle the mountain pass; yet at the same time we must place a ring through the bull's nose, so that his unbridled rage does not lead us over the cliff. Tame the beast and harness his power!

FIFTH

THE MAIDEN'S CARRIAGE

Weaving through the crowd, the young maiden peeks her head out of the carriage, blowing a kiss to the prince and dropping her handkerchief. He was not expecting this and it would be wise to jump at the opportunity before it passes him by.

SIXTH

THE CARRIAGE'S CARGO

Loading every inch of space with goods destined for distant regions, the wise man sets forth with confidence. Now is the time to accept a heavy burden, for we have the strength to carry through to the end.

ALL SIX

THE CARRIAGE DETOURS

The road is impassable, so the wise man detours to a safe, warm place and withdraws from action. It is all we can do at this juncture.

*"Self becomes a reflection
of what we absorb."*

THE JAWS

THE RECEIVER

Thunder in the Mountain

Cook a man a steak and he will eat for an evening. Give him a gun and teach him how to hunt and soon he will be bringing fresh meat to the doorstep. The jaws dictate that it is time to nourish ourselves and gather in close those who make us strong. It may also be the time to observe others, and how they nourish themselves, as this may offer clues about how to find nourishment in our own life. We should now absorb and store power as a bear would gorge before the encroaching winter. The wise man is restrained in speech and frugal in celebration.

頤 THE JAWS

FIRST

JAWS AGAPE!
Never reach for the sky just to surrender.
Do not stand still with jaws agape. There
is no stopping: constant forward motion
is required.

SECOND

IMMATURE JAWS
The boy, thinking he is a man, attempts to
ascend the mountain. Of course, he runs
back to the village at first signs of dusk.
There is inward work to be done before
something like this may be attempted.

THIRD

FORGOING THE JAWS
The aspirant has read too many idealistic
books. He forgoes the middle path and
attempts to find salvation through excess
of self-deprivation. This is not the advised
path at the given moment and no good will
come from such an approach. Wake up!

FOURTH

THE TIGER'S JAWS
The wise man ascends the mountain,
stalking his prey with the gaze of a tiger.
Having found nourishment, he sits still
and allows the world to come to him.

FIFTH

ABNORMAL JAWS
The sky is yellow and the sun is blue.
Things are not as they seem and much
uncertainty looms in the air. Best to stay
where we are, until the situation reverts
to something more normal.

SIXTH

FLEXING THE JAWS
There is a foreign object lodged in the
meat. We recognize this and spit it out
before continuing our meal. If we can push
through the initial trouble, then we will
encounter many good things. It may be
good to go somewhere.

ALL SIX

CLEANING THE JAWS
The tiger spots a herd of gazelles. He
cleans his jaws to prepare for the coming
feast. We should make room to prepare
for what is coming.

*"All show and no strength.
Leaving quickly would be the
only virtue."*

28

THE PEACOCK

EXCESS

A Forest under Water

Excess is Negligence, or perhaps Negligence is Excess.
The peacock spreads its fan wide, proclaiming an
overwhelming display that can be seen for miles
around; sadly, this excess attracts the attention of the
hunter who now fixes the bird in his sights. There is
too much of a good thing, there is no foundation
to support the weight. The wise man gives pause
and reconsiders the simple choice.

大過 THE PEACOCK

THE PEACOCK'S FEATHER
While decorating the house, she decides to
go the extra mile and purchases a bundle
of pricey yet beautiful feathers. That is
to say, if we are going to do something,
then we might as well do it with grace.

SECOND **THE PEACOCK BRIDE**
The withering willow sprouts new
life. The old man takes a young bride.
Such a union may seem strange at first,
but is actually favorable, because their
association has already given rise to much
gossip. Best to close the deal and stand
behind our choice.

THIRD **THE PEACOCK'S DEATH**
The bird has spread its fan too wide, the
hunter draws his bow. We need a better
foundation before we take action.

FOURTH **THE PEACOCK ESCAPES**
Despite the excessive display, the bird
narrowly avoids the approaching arrow
and prances off into the forest. We have
attempted a dangerous course without
adequate support, but somehow are
able to escape unscathed.

FIFTH

THE PEACOCK'S GROOM
The withered willow sprouts a blossom.
Such a thing is beautiful, but how can
it last? The old woman takes a young
husband. Such a thing is tolerated, but
hardly respected.

SIXTH

THE PEACOCK DROWNS
He attempts to walk across the river, but
the water is too high and nearly takes his
life. We are not exactly to blame for this
misfortune, but perhaps we should have
taken a boat?

ALL SIX

THE PEACOCK'S DANCE
Spreading its fan wide, the peacock
performs an alluring dance that moves
the heart of the hunter. So much so that
he puts down his bow and makes an
offering to the illustrious bird.

*"Within the Abyss of Despair
a sincere heart still may not
be sufficient."*

29

THE ABYSS

DARKNESS

Endless Water

習坎

If we stare into the abyss long enough, the abyss will start to stare back at us. Black upon a black river forever flowing with no beginning and no end. Walking along, he falls into a crack. Despair! No quarter is being given, we descend into a struggle to maintain our very existence and must conjure a steadfast fire in our belly and use all means necessary to strike back and free ourselves from the clutch of this encroaching danger. We must now do what we must do, for if we fail there will be no tomorrow.

習坎 THE ABYSS

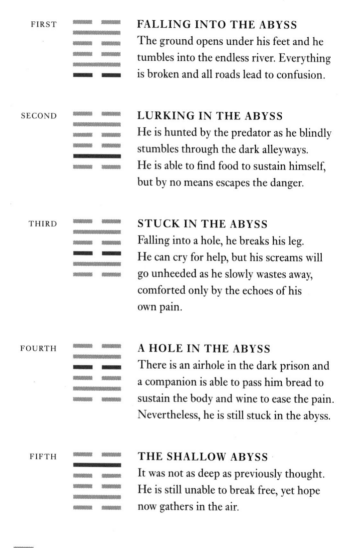

FIRST

FALLING INTO THE ABYSS
The ground opens under his feet and he
tumbles into the endless river. Everything
is broken and all roads lead to confusion.

SECOND

LURKING IN THE ABYSS
He is hunted by the predator as he blindly
stumbles through the dark alleyways.
He is able to find food to sustain himself,
but by no means escapes the danger.

THIRD

STUCK IN THE ABYSS
Falling into a hole, he breaks his leg.
He can cry for help, but his screams will
go unheeded as he slowly wastes away,
comforted only by the echoes of his
own pain.

FOURTH

A HOLE IN THE ABYSS
There is an airhole in the dark prison and
a companion is able to pass him bread to
sustain the body and wine to ease the pain.
Nevertheless, he is still stuck in the abyss.

FIFTH

THE SHALLOW ABYSS
It was not as deep as previously thought.
He is still unable to break free, yet hope
now gathers in the air.

SIXTH

IMPRISONED IN THE ABYSS
He is captured and bound with black
rope. For three years he remains
imprisoned, serving as sustenance
for another's twisted existence.

ALL SIX

**BREAKING FREE FROM
THE ABYSS**
A choir of angels sings as the first light
of the new golden dawn shines through
the bars of his prison. All bonds are
released as he now flies forth toward
that which will be.

*"Clarity with compassion,
the illuminating flame rises twice."*

THE
ARCHANGEL

DIVINE LIGHT

Flaming Arches

The wise man approaches the flaming gates of Heaven, dropping to his knees and intoning a prayer. This is the time of dependence, to be receptive and content to receive assistance from above, while being willing to lend ourselves to those beneath our care. Involving ourselves with the destiny of others will bring assured success. Caring for our neighbor as we care for ourselves will increase our gain a hundredfold.

離 THE ARCHANGEL

FIRST

PRAYING TO THE ARCHANGEL
He speaks a prayer and then approaches
with humility and the utmost respect. In
this way, we shall remain without fault.

SECOND

FOLLOWING THE ARCHANGEL
The angel's steps burn an impression into
the earth, leaving a well-marked trail that
we may follow. The wise man takes this
path, which is known as the middle path –
that is, the way that is balanced, reasonable
and without extremity.

THIRD

THE ARCHANGEL SIGHS
The sound that is not a sound is heard
(or perhaps not heard) as the sun touches
the mountain. Young men are advised to
remain silent and enjoy the sunset while
it lasts, for night is coming soon. Things
were at peace, but now be prepared for
some serious challenges.

FOURTH

THE ARCHANGEL'S JUDGMENT
It came with a flurry of brilliance, bringing
momentary elation. But just as it came,
how quickly it is cast away. Best now to let
go, for it will not return anytime soon.

FIFTH

THE ARCHANGEL'S FEATHER
Overwhelmed by this or that, the wise man opens his floodgates and allows the tears to tumble forth. By regretting our actions and wanting to make things right, we will find forgiveness from above.

SIXTH

THE ARCHANGEL'S SWORD
Taking a deep breath and donning his armor, the wise man marches forth to destroy that which opposes the law of his word. After he defeats the leader, he bestows compassion upon the followers and attempts to recruit them into his own army.

ALL SIX

THE ARCHANGEL FALLS
A storm brews in Heaven as the winds of chaos rage forth and overwhelm the wise man. Such is the nature of the tides of creation. Best now to hunker down and limit the damage.

*"Seizing the initiative:
penetration for the sake
of submission."*

THE LOVER

ATTRACTION

Lake upon the Mountain

His eyes open wide with passion as the blood pumps and butterflies dance in the stomach. That which was dead is now reborn as that which we desire now becomes clear like the day. He moves toward her with confidence and a burning longing as the river touches the sea. The man lends support to the woman and accepts her burden as the wise man stimulates people's hearts with words of poetry and wisdom. This is a time to observe and understand that which causes us pleasure or pain and to act with confidence to bear the fruits of our will.

咸 THE LOVER

FIRST

GREATER THAN THE LOVER
Although he has a burning in his loins,
he overcomes this through the logic of the
mind to focus on outward matters. There
are other things that must be done before
this love may be tended.

SECOND

RESTRAINING THE LOVE
Oh how he burns to reach out to her, but
now is not the time. Best to bow to the
will of others and hold our desire in check.
The wise man does not leave the comforts
of his own home.

THIRD

THE LOVER IS LEASHED
Diving too far, too deep into the river
of passion, he awakes to find himself
under collar and chain. A foolish person
has gained undue influence, and may be
leading us to ruin. Best to be done with
this person and get as far away as possible.
Do we have the strength to escape?

FOURTH

THE LOVER MUST CHOOSE

Being wooed by scores of handmaidens,
the prince is able to choose only one upon
which to bestow his affection. He will
win her hand and satisfy his love through
confident persistence, but at the same
time alienate the rest of the women. Such
a thing may be deemed necessary by the
tides of creation: we should put the others
out of mind.

FIFTH

THE LOVER FAILS

We really try our best, but we are just not
strong enough to impose the extent of
our will. Let all pass and prepare for
another day!

SIXTH

FOILING THE LOVER

Everything was in accord, but he kept
talking and ruined the whole thing. Best
to keep our mouth closed and speak with
our action.

ALL SIX

THE LOVER ATTAINS

He has attained that which he seeks, and
a calculated retreat is in order; but this
is now a good thing!

"Movement and duration.
Marriage of the responsibilities."

THE
MARATHON

LONG DISTANCE

Thunder and Wind

Long-distance runner, be prepared to embark upon
a task of epic proportions. The marathon is a time to
focus upon a long-term goal, employing the virtue of
consistency. It is good to choose a goal or destination
and begin trudging forward one step at a time,
always confident that we will achieve our desire.
This is the time of balance and diligent work.

FIRST

POSITIONING FOR THE MARATHON

He focused all his attention trying to get into position at the starting line, so that he missed the starting gun.

SECOND

PACING THE MARATHON

He understands that it is a long race and paces his steps accordingly so as to not waste his energy. The wise man avoids extremes of any kind and follows the middle path.

THIRD

CHEATING AT THE MARATHON

He attempts to play foul and is spotted by the other runners. They turn away from him in disgust. This was his own choice.

FOURTH

ILL-SUITED FOR THE MARATHON

He would be better off behind a desk! Try as we might, there are just some things we will never be good at. The wise man devotes his attention to finding a task more suited to his temperament.

FIFTH

THE MARATHON OF THE WISE
Those who are diligent and even of temperament shall find success with focused determination, while those who are impulsive and still lacking in maturity of character shall find all roads blocked.

SIXTH

STRAINING AT THE MARATHON
Too much, too fast. He strains a tendon and must drop out of the race. He should have paced himself.

ALL SIX

FINISHING THE MARATHON
He did not come in first, he did not come in last. Overall, it was quite a successful race. But the season has just begun and there is another race next week. Good work! Keep moving forward.

*"Without anger, allowing
darkness to pass,
turning the eye inward."*

THE HERMIT

WITHDRAWAL

Mountain under the Sky

We have been correct in our pushing, but we must understand that every action will also have a reaction. That said, we shall perform a calculated and joyful withdrawal from current circumstances. In this way, we may cultivate what we have gained, as a gardener would a newly acquired sapling. The hermit withdraws to the mountain in a blissful state, excited about the wisdom gained and the time he will have to allow it to blossom within his being. That said, we are advised to leave other people to their own devices and withdraw!

FIRST

THE HERMIT IS STUCK
He thought to dig himself a hole in which
to withdraw, but now he is stuck in the
hole! The wise man yields, but not by
extremes. Remember, after the yielding
is finished, we still have to return.

SECOND

THE HERMIT'S KNOT
Tying and binding our affairs with a
steadfast will presages assured success.
The wise man ties up all loose affairs
and binds the rest with iron before he
withdraws. No quarter should be given.

THIRD

THE FATIGUED HERMIT
He yields not out of joy, but rather out of
overwhelming fatigue. There is no success
in such a thing. Instead of withdrawing,
the wise man will focus on non-stressful
associates such as servants and lovers.

FOURTH

THE CALCULATING HERMIT
The wise man now withdraws for good
reason as those of mean temperament
engage in self-destructive activities.
He observes this from the shadows and
returns to claim the territory after the
others have exhausted their will from
fighting each other.

FIFTH

THE HONORABLE HERMIT
Every action he takes is without fault and
in consideration of all people. Following
such an honorable path now dictates
a withdrawal.

SIXTH

THE HERMIT RETIRES
Everything is golden and finished.
The wise man ties up loose ends, says
his goodbyes and ventures forth to
construct his dream home upon the
mountain. There should be no doubt
in this, for all omens are favorable.

ALL SIX

THE HERMIT RETURNS
Being rich in all things, the wise man
re-enters the marketplace and distributes
his goods and power freely to those who
may ask. Now is the joyful time of giving
and drawing people inward.

"Power to move, power to change.
Forget not the wisdom of the just."

THE HORNS

POWER

Thunder in the Sky

The goat digs in his heels and charges with great force at the imminent hedge. This is the time to exercise our will through a forceful and dramatic display. We shall put our head down and charge without doubt toward the stated goal. If anything should get in our way, then it will have to deal with the stubborn and fearsome power of the horns. The wise man knows that he is correct and not afraid to exercise his will.

大壯 THE HORNS

FIRST

INFANT HORNS
Our power is not yet fully blossomed.
If we advance now, we will soon find that
we do not possess enough strength to carry
things to completion. The wise man shall
wait until he is at the height of his power
to advance.

SECOND

LOWERING THE HORNS
Charging toward our goal with confidence
will bring success. The wise man knows
that few are able to withstand the great
power of the horns.

THIRD

RESTRAINING THE HORNS
Oh, how he wants to charge forth, but
he notices a barb entangled in the hedge.
Some enemy has placed it there to trick us!
To persist as planned would mean getting
stuck in the hedge. Better to holster the
horns and use delicate skill and cunning
to remove the barb.

FOURTH

FREEING THE HORNS
Although he is presently stuck, he
continues to struggle with ferocity and is
able to free himself. Regaining his strength,
he is able to charge forth as before.

FIFTH

MISUSING THE HORNS

The uneducated will charge at anything that is bright and shiny. The wise man understands that sometimes the best action is non-action and considers carefully before resorting to force.

SIXTH

THE HORNS ENTANGLED

He came in at the wrong angle and got his horns stuck in the hedge. Do not despair. Could it perhaps be that the shame of this minor misfortune is a necessary step in the process of waking up and learning to take responsibility for ourselves?

ALL SIX

RESTING THE HORNS

There is nowhere to go and nothing to do. The hedge in the distance is but an illusion or perhaps a trap of the mind attempting to draw us away from the great wealth we already possess. Best that we remain where we are and watch the world unfold before our eyes.

"Progress is hastened owing to royal status. One shall not refuse gifts."

THE PRINCE

RADIANCE

A Pillar of Flame

Like a pillar of flame in the desert, we shine brightly
for all to see. The prince is given an illustrious steed
and granted audience three times in one day! The wise
man understands that good things sometimes come in
threes and accepts the gifts that aid him in his progress.
Now is the time to be gracious and bold in our actions
for we have the support of our admirers.

晉　THE PRINCE

THE LIBERAL PRINCE

Even though there is still mistrust,
he will give freely without hope of
recompensation. Things may change in
the near future, so it is best to maintain
relationships and not burn any bridges.

THE PRINCE'S MOTHER

Although there seems to be sorrow at
whatever action we take, we must continue
to trudge forward. Following the wisdom
of an elder woman will bring clarity to
the situation.

THE PRINCE RIDES FORTH

He gathers his companions and raises
his banners. The wise man picks a
star, follows it and rides forth with
determination to achieve his objective.

THE PRINCE MUST WAIT

The king still lives and the prince has
not yet completed his education. The
wise man does not attempt to rise above
his station before the appointed time
has come.

FIFTH

THE SELFLESS PRINCE
He makes a decision and carries it to the end without care for loss or gain. Doing what we must do, in the end we will find blessings.

SIXTH

THE PRINCE'S CHARGE
Showing signs of immaturity, he charges recklessly against the enemy. He does this not so much for the conflict, but rather for the lust of battle. War is serious and should only be carried out with a concrete objective. The wise man will press against an enemy, but also knows to stop once he has achieved his goal.

ALL SIX

THE HUMBLE PRINCE
Removing his gold chains and donning the clothing of the common man, the prince is able to walk thorough the city without notice. It would be best now not to attract too much attention.

"*Main radiance inward; yet
outward, better presumed dead.*"

THE MASK

DRAPING

Fire Hidden in the Earth

明夷

Entering into the earth, the fire will be extinguished.
The mask is like the eclipse. This is a quiet, perhaps
injurious time when it is best to subdue our own power
and yield to others. It is a time to conceal who we are
and our true intentions by allowing others to take the
limelight as we watch patiently from the shadows.
To do otherwise would bring harm to ourselves.

明夷 THE MASK

FIRST

THE MASK OF DILIGENCE
Donning the mask, he is forced to fold in
his wings and return to the grotto. There is
work to be done and this should be tackled
with the utmost attention. This may mean
working three days straight, with little
pause for food or sleep. The wise man
gets done what must be done and ignores
others' foolish comments regarding the
diligence of his work.

SECOND

THE MASK OF HASTE
Running too fast, he falls down and
injures his left leg. Luckily there is
a horse nearby, which he mounts to
complete his emergency duties. Although
he is hurt, the wise man searches for
and makes use of help to accomplish
his immediate tasks. Finish it!

THIRD

THE MASK OF MADNESS
Wounded while in the south, he pushes
through to capture the enemy. At this
point, the wise man will step back and
view the situation with a balanced mind, so
as to not become deluded by compulsions
of madness that would destroy what has
already been accomplished.

FOURTH

THE MASK OF THE HEART
Locking left eye to left eye, he sees deep into another and perceives a darkened heart. To persist shall bring an infection of ill will in our hearts. Do what thou wilt and accept the consequences.

FIFTH

LIGHT THROUGH THE MASK
Although he is injured, he continues to push forward. His light shines, even through the darkness. We will be rewarded if we remain steadfast with honorable intention.

SIXTH

THE BLACK MASK
Without even holes for eyes! The former ruler transgressed the divine law and was bound with an impenetrable mask. Nothing can be done except weep or perhaps sing a sad song.

ALL SIX

THE WARRIOR'S MASK
Donning the warrior's mask and iron gauntlets, he formulates strategies to crush his enemy. No quarter should be given. It is advised to keep the battle on the home turf, by setting a trap and drawing the enemy inward, causing him to overextend his resources.

"Forming foundations that cannot be shaken and being sincere in word and duty."

THE FAMILY

THE HEARTH

Wind Rising from Fire

The family is a mechanism that functions properly when each member keeps to their assigned place. A woman's place is within, a man's without. Sons should obey their fathers and daughters after their mother. When these roles are accepted with sincerity, the family runs as a single entity and is bestowed blessings from above. It is advised for women to embrace the archetypal feminine and to proceed in this manner, while men are advised to remain diligent, waiting for the command of the one they serve.

FIRST

THE MOUNTAINOUS FAMILY
Being complete unto itself, the family
resides in an isolated part of the
mountains. Already having everything
that he needs to be whole, the wise man
turns his attention inward and enjoys
everyday affairs.

SECOND

ONLY THE FAMILY
Everything on the outside is broken, but
the family remains joyful. External affairs
may bring complications; better to focus
attention inward toward the hearth.

THIRD

THE FATHER'S FAMILY
It is the father's role to discipline and
speak sharply when required. In this
way, he prunes the weeds and maintains
a harmonious household. However, if
the woman or child attempts to fill this
authoritative role, disaster shall strike.
For this would surely put things out
of balance.

FOURTH

THE WELL-OILED FAMILY
Running smoothly through the daily
routines will bring great fortune to the
family. The wise man tends his garden
with a joyful smile.

FIFTH

LOVE OF THE FAMILY
Drawing close to those around him,
the wise one bestows and accepts love.
It is that simple!

SIXTH

THE EVOLVING FAMILY
Giving himself to frequent self-
examination, the wise man recognizes
and works through his faults. Only
through the constant cycle of renewal
may a family remain whole and function
as a single entity.

ALL SIX

SACRIFICING FOR THE FAMILY
Like a holiday dinner with all those
relatives we abhor to see, or perhaps a
nail-biting favor, sometimes we must put
our own wishes aside and do what is best
for the family.

*"In opposition there is no agreement,
yet still no cause for conflict."*

THE
STRANGER

DESERTED

The Lake of Fire

People are strange, when you are a stranger. Everything seems so distant, everything is the opposite of ourselves. Feelings of disconnection may arise. This is a time of waiting in which we do not possess the power to accomplish great things. However, know that the stranger is protected from above and will be able to find sustenance in small things. Instead of reaching out to the people who would label him "strange", the wise man cultivates his "difference" – and opens his eyes to see those of a similar temperament gather around him.

FIRST

THE STRANGER'S NEMESIS
Although we may lose something, we
should not chase this horse: it will return
of its own accord. During this time, we
may receive a visit from a wicked man,
attempting to sow his destructive seed.
We should not fight, send away or accept
this visitor. Rather, politely ignore him
and he will leave of his own accord.
In this way, we remain faultless.

SECOND

THE STRANGER'S LORD
Walking the streets after hours, he
encounters his lord in a narrow alleyway.
By doing this, he causes his superior a
small trouble. We should not feel regret
or shame for this encounter, as it was not
our fault and will quickly be forgotten.

THIRD

THE STRANGER IS BEATEN
He watches helplessly as fools attack in
the night, slicing his nose and taking his
valuables. What bad luck! Rest assured, if
we remain steadfast and let this regression
pass, it will quickly be forgotten.

FOURTH

THE STRANGER'S HUSBAND
She was so lonely and the neighbors
thought her quite peculiar. Blessed be,
for she soon met a respectable man,

who although he had faults of his own
tried his best and turned out to be quite
the good husband.

FIFTH

THE STRANGER LEADS
If we have one stranger, he will be
considered crazy. Two strangers and then
we have a marriage. Ten strangers and
then we have a party. One hundred or
more strangers and we are bordering
on a religion. The wise man gathers the
like-minded around him.

SIXTH

THE STRANGER'S DEMON
Wandering lost and lonely through the
night, he encounters a demon upon the
road. At first he wanted to attack, but then
reconsidered the situation and the nature
of demons. That said, he simply waited
for the rain, which naturally banished the
foe. The wise man waits for doubt to be
vanquished before proceeding.

ALL SIX

THE STRANGER COMES HOME
Exhausted from wandering alone, the
stranger returns home to try to create
a normal life.

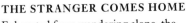

"The Way is broken.
Advice should be well heeded."

39

THE RAVEN

TROUBLE

A Mountain under Water

The raven itself is not an unfortunate omen: actually it is quite the helpful little bird. For it carries the burdensome task of warning about upcoming troubles. We should be on our guard, for an unexpected adversary may be coming our way. The raven advises us to concentrate attention on the south and the west, while avoiding all things east and north. It would also be positive to take counsel from a wise elder and to heed their words.

蹇　THE RAVEN

THE RAVEN PERCHES
The raven patiently waits on the branch.
Going anywhere will bring much trouble.
At this time, it is better to come than to
go. The wise man cultivates patience.

THE RAVEN'S CLAW
There is a thorn stuck in the claw.
Someone under our care may soon
encounter trouble. We are not to blame
for this, and really there is not much
we can do.

THE RAVEN CIRCLES BACK
To continue to move forward will bring
travesty; better to turn back. By doing so,
we bring the woman much happiness.

THE RAVEN'S NEST
We may think that we need to move
forward to accomplish our aims. But this
will just lead to disaster. Rest assured,
there are people coming in our direction
who will offer assistance as we remain in
the background.

FIFTH

THE RAVEN'S FRIEND
Every trouble has its underlying reason.
We awake to find ourselves buried deep in
a pile of thick mud. Rest assured, a friend
will soon arrive to help us out of this mess.

SIXTH

THE EYE OF THE RAVEN
To go forward will bring disaster. Better
to come back and take counsel from
a wise elder.

ALL SIX

THE RAVEN'S EGG
Out of the egg comes new life. Rejoice,
for this is the time of birth. Yet we must
still take care to make preparations for
the fresh trials ahead.

*"Advance toward the future
or retreat toward the past.
The present is now history."*

THE ARROW

RELEASE

Thunder and Rain

The bow string hums as the arrow whizzes forth into the air. After an excruciating build-up, the heavens open to bring a joyous rain. The arrow is the time of release, to let go and pass from the place where we now reside. If there is something to gain by advancing, then we should do so with the utmost force and haste. On the other hand, if there is really nothing to gain, then a calculated retreat would be in order. Regardless, we can no longer stay where we are now. The wise man praises all things south and west while avoiding those east and north.

解　THE ARROW

FIRST

THE STRAIGHT ARROW
By following conventions and remaining
careful to avoid simple mistakes, we shall
find success in our undertaking.

SECOND

THREE BIRDS WITH ONE ARROW
Out of necessity, the hunter takes the
risky shot and transfixes three pheasants
with a single arrow. Now is the time to
take a chance, for the omens are in accord.

THIRD

THE JEWELED ARROW
Although it may be nice to look at, the
jeweled arrow gives a bad shot at best and
will only attract the attention of thieves
and hooligans. The wise man discards
vanity and gravitates toward that which
is functional.

FOURTH

THE ARROW IS DROPPED
Like a clown, he messes everything up –
though really, this is more humorous
than calamitous. Rest assured, a friend
will soon arrive to set things straight.

FIFTH

THE ARROW MASTER
The shot is too difficult for the common man; the master steps forth and draws his bow. If we are in command of this situation, then we should go forward. If not, then it would be best to follow the lead of he who holds the reins.

SIXTH

THE ARROW FINDS FLESH
Piercing through the skin, the arrow brings down a prized bird. This elates the hunter and separates him from the pack. The wise man cultivates the hunter's confidence and separates himself from the affairs of lesser men.

ALL SIX

SHEATHING THE ARROW
There is too much going on for us to advance safely. Better to consolidate the present position, for something may be brewing that we are not aware of.

"*Reduce, even against better judgment. Say less and be diligent in work.*"

PRUNING

REDUCING

Lake under the Mountain

The bushes have grown too large and spill onto the
street. This is a time of reduction, the time to take
inventory of the players and circumstances and cut
away that which is not needed. By doing so, we allow
for fresh growth. If there is doubt about what to prune,
then we should begin with the most basic element.

損 PRUNING

FIRST

A HASTY PRUNING
There is no harm in accomplishing
work quickly, as long as this does not
affect the quality of the work. The wise
man waits for the acknowledgment of his
superiors before stamping his seal upon
the project.

SECOND

NO PRUNING TODAY
Instead of clipping the bushes, he
augments what is already there by
posting a stake to hold them upright.

THIRD

PRUNING THE COMPANIONS
Three is a crowd, and with two, all
they do is look at each other. Better to
set forth alone with the confidence that
a valuable companion will be met upon
the road.

FOURTH

PRUNING THE THORNS
Overwhelmed by a score of various
troubles, the wise man takes a deep breath
and methodically begins tackling his
adversaries one by one. He begins with
what is easiest to remedy.

FIFTH

REWARD FOR THE PRUNING
While he is working diligently, someone
presents him with a wonderful gift. This
should not be refused. The wise man
accepts what is offered.

SIXTH

AN HONORABLE PRUNING
Pulling the weeds, he takes care not to
harm the flowers. An action or gain can
only be considered faultless if it does
not harm another in the process. At
this juncture, the wise man turns his
attention away from family and focuses
on subordinates.

ALL SIX

AFTER THE PRUNING
After the work is done and the first
rains fall, life shoots forth like an
excitable young bull. Charge forward
with confidence.

"Movement, increase and sound.
Travel is advised."

42

THE COIN

MILESTONE

Wind and Thunder

This is a time to recognize, accomplish and receive reward for concrete tasks. If there is a bridge, then we should cross. If there is potential, backed by a solid, logical foundation, then we should proceed. If we have no plan, then now is the time to expend resources and formulate one. If something is good, then we shall imitate it; if something is broken, then we shall fix it.

益 THE COIN

FIRST

SPENDING THE COIN
Purchasing the materials of highest
quality will lead to a solid foundation and
a house that will last many generations.
If we treat our workers with respect and
occasionally buy them lunch, then they
will be happy to work long hours to help
us achieve our goals.

SECOND

ACCEPTING THE COIN
Someone came from the outside and
bestowed upon us an unexpected gift.
They would not accept no for an answer.
This gift should be accepted graciously
and be put to good use.

THIRD

THE BLACK COIN
Although his original intentions were
good, he deviated, and dubious means
were used to gain the coin. If we go to
another now and pledge our loyalty, then
all shall be forgiven.

FOURTH

TRUSTED WITH THE COIN
Openly walking to the center of the sphere,
he declares his intention to serve the
public. It is good now to be trusted with
heavy burdens, for we have the strength
to carry a project through to completion.

FIFTH

TRUSTING THE COIN
Many wheels turn of which we are unaware. The wise man does not ask questions; rather, he moves forward with faith and confidence. Although we may be blind, know that the road is straight and clear.

SIXTH

THE PREJUDICED COIN
Recalling the prejudices of the old guard, he did not treat someone with proper respect and incurred the hatred of another clan. This is one of those things that could have been so easily avoided.

ALL SIX

INVESTING THE COIN
Now is the time to focus upon distant goals and make investments for the long run. The farmer plants his crops in spring to harvest in the fall.

"Distribution of accumulation, measured and weighted."

43

THE
PROCLAMATION

RESOLUTION

A Lake Drawn towards the Sky

The proclamation to the people should be a calculated affair. Consider this a surgical strike – it should be done not for peace of mind, but rather to instill a particular emotion in the people. That said, information should be dispersed only according to necessity. And the objective should be to charm, not to frighten: words shall be melodious, swords shall remain sheathed. The wise man first resolves in his own heart what must be done, then he announces it to the people and sets forth with unwavering courage.

FIRST

THE HOLLOW PROCLAMATION
Thinking he could impress the people, he took upon himself a task too momentous to complete. He rode forth and returned in shame. The wise man carefully measures his ability before committing to a task.

SECOND

BACKING UP THE PROCLAMATION
He who speaks of action must follow through to completion. If we fear carrying through what we have started, we shall purchase guns and knives to silence these fears of inadequacy. The wise man knows no fear.

THIRD

THE PRIDEFUL PROCLAMATION
Making a big show of his strength, he continued to walk alone even though it was raining. Eventually he got stuck in the mud – although in the end nobody could point a finger.

FOURTH

THE BEATEN PROCLAMATION
He was not strong enough to complete the task and now wanders confused and hesitant through the desert. A caravan offers assistance, but this he refuses because he is too proud to follow another's lead. Is this the most intelligent path?

FIFTH

EKING OUT THE PROCLAMATION

Although a minor obstacle presents itself, he continues forward with unwavering tenacity. In the end, he achieves what he desires, though perhaps not in the smoothest way.

SIXTH

THE PROCLAMATION FAILS

He thought that it was completed, but one step away from the finish, unexpected calamity happened and the whole thing failed. The wise man carries affairs through to the bitter end and knows that it is not over until it is over.

ALL SIX

THE LETTER OF THE PROCLAMATION

When seeking counsel, he looks back at what he has already declared and follows this scripted path to the end. We already have all the information we need; now it is just a matter of doing the job and doing it well.

*"Darkness beckons.
We may choose to disperse
or penetrate."*

THE GATE

THE MISTRESS

The Winds of Heaven

They are drawn to each other at first sight as he takes her hand and knows that it is better not to ask her name. This is a time of contact or momentary union. Enjoy it, gain from the experience, using it as a catalyst to draw strength from the source. However, we must not try to make anything lasting, for this path will lead straight into the spider's web.

 THE GATE

FIRST

STRUGGLING TOWARD THE GATE

So many troubles upon the road, but he continues to push forward even if this means dragging along his companions. Rejoice, for the gate will soon be reached, but not before another suffers misfortune upon the same road.

SECOND

BARRING THE GATE

He has much to give, but refuses to entertain guests. Such selfishness may rebound on him and bite him in the back.

THIRD

APPROACHING THE GATE

His clothes are now rags and he walks with a limp. Rejoice, for the one-eyed monk has finally reached the jade gate. There may be trouble, but if we are steadfast, then we shall reach our goal.

FOURTH

HIDING FROM THE GATE

His power is spent and he has nothing left to give. He isolates himself. This disconnection from people may not be a good thing, as there is no one who can assist us.

FIFTH

INSIDE THE GATE
From the outside, it was nothing
spectacular, but as he entered, the gate
closed behind him and quite a magnificent
sight was seen. There is a hidden beauty
at work that gives its assistance subtly,
owing to shyness.

SIXTH

EXHAUSTION AT THE GATE
He has done all that he can do and fumbles
helplessly at the gate. We have done our
best: it is not our fault that we failed.

ALL SIX

A CRACK IN THE GATE
The gate does not open completely, but
only by a hair. He should accept what
is given with grace, while at the same
time subtly positioning himself to gain
deeper entry.

*"Gathering closely,
watchful of the perimeter."*

THE COUNCIL

GATHERING

Lake upon the Earth

People gather to consult about the state of affairs and make a decision in agreement with each other. This is a time to come together and request advice from a grouping of people, as many minds may be able to perceive that which is cloudy to the one. It may also be time to offer a sacrifice to something greater than ourselves for the sake of furthering our cause. The wise man chooses a star and charts its course.

FIRST

THE COUNCIL INDECISIVE

They start and stop and really get nowhere. Perhaps there is fear about taking action? This should be overcome and action taken.

SECOND

JOINING THE COUNCIL

He confidently steps into the hall and asks for assistance from the council. Now is the time to be drawn into the affairs of others while making the correct sacrifice as price of admission.

THIRD

THE MOURNFUL COUNCIL

They all look so sad and prefer to mourn rather than take action. This is fine, and if action is taken, then it should be with a gentle hand.

FOURTH

THE COUNCIL CELEBRATES

All are in agreement and a firm decision has been made. Rejoice, for now it is just a matter of working out the details.

FIFTH

THE COUNCIL IN DISPUTE
They agree to listen to his words, for
he carries much respect, but he does
not yet have the power to convince them
of his cause. He should persist in his
path until he feels that he has done all
that he can.

SIXTH

THE COUNCIL SIGHS
Things are going wrong, although this is
not our fault. Nevertheless, there is not
much else to do but sigh and let it pass.

ALL SIX

THE CONFIDENT COUNCIL
Knowing that his cause is righteous and
honorable, he steps forward and wins the
people's support. Now is the time to be
sincere and accurate with our words.

"Pushing small things upward
shall evolve into that which is great."

GROWTH

SAPLING

A Tree Pushing through the Earth

The trees grow upward from the earth, beginning
as saplings and eventually becoming towering legends.
The wise man ascends the mountain step by step,
knowing that all good things come in good time. If
there are doubts, then we should take counsel from an
elder to banish this anxiety. Furthermore, matters in
the southern realm will bring assured success.

升　GROWTH

FIRST

A CERTAIN GROWTH
Following time-honored convention for
the care of the sapling will surely lead to
a healthy tree. Those who stand above us
support and agree with our actions.

SECOND

SACRIFICING FOR THE GROWTH
Just as a parent gives a part of themselves
to nurture the child, we should now make
a sacrifice to nurture our objective. It is
now time to concentrate on the gentle,
spiritual aspects of our life.

THIRD

TRANSPLANTING THE GROWTH
The tree has grown too large for its pot.
It is time to transplant it to the forest.
Good things will come as long as we create
sufficient space in our life to accept them.

FOURTH

GROWTH ON THE MOUNTAIN
Following tradition, he cares for the old
tree on the mountain. Now is the time
to accept the ways of our elders, for they
have already been proven and will lead
to assured success.

FIFTH

INCREMENTAL GROWTH

Good things are coming, but progress must be made step by step. Have no fear for what lies ahead, but rather focus on the step before us. The path will lead through the forest.

SIXTH

A BLIND GROWTH

He wants it so badly that he works all through the night and long past the dawn. This way of working may help us to achieve our objective, but at the same time may lead to loss of money.

ALL SIX

OBSERVING THE GROWTH

There is still much to be done, but perhaps we do not possess all the required information? Now is the time to step back and assess the situation from a balanced perspective, so that we may understand it better before we take action.

"*Even the truth is now forsaken.*
Best that all movements now
turn inward."

47

THE SHADOW

WEARINESS

A Dry Lake

The shadow follows him everywhere he goes, creating
difficulty after difficulty. He is weary, but if he persists
with righteous intention, then he will achieve his objective
despite the adversary. Now is the time for action, not
words; for enough words have already been spoken and to
speak more will just detract from our cause. The wise man
understands that the shadow is being cast from something
hidden. He attempts to unearth the root of the problem,
even if this means taking an extraordinary risk.

FIRST

THE SHADOW OVERCOMES
The adversary is too great and overcomes him. There is nothing we can do to improve the situation. The wise man resigns himself to failure and begins to focus on new things.

SECOND

THE SHADOW OF INDULGENCE
He creates problems for himself through excessive indulgence in food and drink. All seems lost until a distinguished man arrives. It is advised to make sacrifice to this man and ask for his assistance in improving the situation.

THIRD

THE SHADOW OF HIS WIFE
Everything was going wrong and he could find nothing to lean upon. He returned to his home to find his wife gone too. The best thing about hitting the very bottom is that there is only one way to go!

FOURTH

THE SHADOW OF PRESUMPTION
Placing too much hope in another will lead to failure. Best to plan to weather this trouble alone. Our power is weak, and results will be achieved very slowly until we can regain our confidence.

FIFTH

THE SHADOW OF HIS LORD
We have insulted one who stands above
us and are now receiving due punishment.
Nothing will be achieved in the near
future, but if we are humble and offer a
sacrifice, we may be able to lift ourselves
out of this situation.

SIXTH

REGRETTING THE SHADOW
He awakes to realize that his life is in
disarray and that it is mostly his own fault.
If he regrets his past actions, and does
his best to be an honorable man, then
resolution will be found.

ALL SIX

ACCEPTING THE SHADOW
It is useless to fight, but perhaps we can
take what we have and turn it around to
work in our favor? Perhaps.

*"Proper preparations in order
to draw direct from the source."*

THE WELL

THE SOURCE

Water Held in Wood

A city may be moved, but not a well. Always there in one
place as a source of nourishment, the well draws people from
miles around to give subsistence. This is a time to cultivate
permanence; setting roots and digging deep, we will find our
success. Yet we must still be on guard, for although the well
is ever plentiful, sometimes the rope is too short to draw the
awaiting water. If this should occur, then the wise man will
use all means necessary to put things right.

 THE WELL

FIRST

THE MUDDY WELL
The well is very old and the water is not drinkable. The wise man resigns himself to failure and searches for new horizons.

SECOND

THE LEAKY WELL
We have left too many loose ends lying around and now they all gather to thwart our cause. We should pay more attention to details and clean up our messes.

THIRD

THE UNUSED WELL
The water is sparkling clean, yet he does not drink and ends up going thirsty. We are not using the presented opportunities to their greatest potential. The wise man makes good use of what is offered.

FOURTH

THE WELL UNDER REPAIR
Masons work diligently as the wise man waits patiently with empty pitcher. There will be a delay in our project, but this is a good thing, as matters must be put in correct order before we may proceed.

FIFTH

THE DELICIOUS WELL
The water is cool and tastes like a
fresh mountain spring. We should have
sufficient strength to accomplish our
objective, as we now have many things
in our favor.

SIXTH

THE WELL ROPE
The rope to pull water lays in open coils
all ready to be used. All the groundwork
has been laid. All we must do now is go
through the motions.

ALL SIX

DISMANTLING THE WELL
Although there still may be water, he
dismantles the well for materials that
are desperately needed for another
purpose. We may need to sacrifice
something that is still useful.

"Young overtakes old.
One stands alone as the maker
of change."

THE
REVOLUTION

CHANGE

Boiling Water

Revolution! Drastic change! Nobody has faith in it until the day of completion. The wise man ignores the doubters and presses forward with his cause. The revolution is the time to choose a side, to believe in a cause and to press forward with absolute determination. Do not expect support from the people, for the cause is risky and they are still fearful. But know that after the work is completed, we will have the full support of the populace.

革 THE REVOLUTION

FIRST

**STRENGTHENING
THE REVOLUTION**
We do not yet have the necessary strength
to carry forward our plans. Better now
to strengthen the foundation with ropes
and knots.

SECOND

**WAITING FOR THE
REVOLUTION**
To advance now would bring defeat.
Better to wait until the revolution has
been completed. By waiting and then
advancing when the message "All clear"
is given, the wise man finds unexpected
good fortune.

THIRD

TALK OF THE REVOLUTION
While change is still no more than an idea,
it would be wise to wait. However, after
the idea has been discussed three times,
then we should press forward with
determination and fury.

FOURTH

**SUPPORT FOR THE
REVOLUTION**
The people agree that it would be for
the best to support the institution of
a new government. This is the time for
a new way of doing things.

FIFTH

REVOLUTION OF THE TIGER
He charges toward his objective with
self-assurance and uncanny brilliance.
Nothing can stop us now. Our confidence
is so great that there is really no need to
consult the oracle.

SIXTH

REVOLUTION OF THE LEOPARD
Leading with the swift grace of a leopard,
those on the other side promptly switch
their allegiance to his cause. Now that this
is done, he does not advance further, but
rather consolidates the present position.

ALL SIX

**A STRANGER TO
THE REVOLUTION**
We seem to have missed the moment and
there is much going on of which we are
not aware. Instead of wasting our energy,
trying to join this cause, perhaps it is
better to direct our attention closer to
our power-base.

"Sacrifice that which is sacred and bring together that which is dear."

THE
CAULDRON

SACRIFICE

Burning Wood

The cauldron is used to cook the sacrifice or meal for all. It is now time to make hard decisions and give up something we prize for the sake of furthering our cause. We shall give this thing freely and without regret, for this is the only way it can assist us. A sacrifice is only a sacrifice if it is something that we love. The wise man spends all day preparing a meal and invites the villagers to his home for the offering.

FIRST

OVERTURNING THE CAULDRON
The meat is spoiled and must be disposed of. It is not shameful to dispose of something that is no longer of use to us. His wife is infertile; he takes a concubine to bear him a child.

SECOND

THE IRON CAULDRON
The foundations in place are unshakable. Our will is steadfast and our enemies have encountered unforeseen trouble.

THIRD

THE CAULDRON'S HANDLES
The handles are missing and we are unable to offer what we have prepared. Sad that such a thing should go to waste. This happened because we spent too much time reminiscing about the past. In the end, rain will come and make everything right.

FOURTH

THE CAULDRON'S LEGS
The legs snap and the sacrifice spills over, spoiling our clothes. Through gross carelessness, he not only lost something, but also created additional trouble for himself.

FIFTH

THE GOLDEN CAULDRON
Our past mishaps have been resolved
to the point where everything is in better
standing than previously. It is time to be
persistent, yet civilized.

SIXTH

THE JADE CAULDRON
She approaches wearing a white silk
gown. He knows that if he can have
her, then the rest of the world would be
nothing but his playpen. Go for it, young
lion; never keep a woman waiting.

ALL SIX

THE FAMILY'S CAULDRON
Cooking the sacrifice, he calls in his
family and cultivates the virtue of the
home. It is best to pay attention now
to the simple things of life.

*"Shock from eight directions,
yet the cup does not spill."*

THE ALARM

SHOCK

Endless Thunder

The alarm sounds with a terrible and frightening shock, lifting people from their seats and sending them running for miles around. In truth, this should not be a time for fright, but rather a time to awaken. The wise man stands coolly in the midst of Chaos, maintaining his balance and taking care not to spill the wine, for he knows that it is just an illusion. Awake! Good things are coming if we remain steadfast.

震 THE ALARM

FIRST

THE FALSE ALARM
Thunder booms in the sky, at first
prompting people to fright. This fear
soon transforms to joy as they perform
the much-needed rain dance.

SECOND

HEEDING THE ALARM
Sirens roar and to this we must take heed.
We should drop whatever we are doing
and flee to the hills for seven days and
seven nights. We should not reminisce
about what was left behind, for it will be
regained when we return.

THIRD

THE EXCESSIVE ALARM
The bell is loud, constant and annoying:
perhaps it is trying to tell us something?
Although it is normally best to be calm
and civil, now is the time to emulate
this alarm.

FOURTH

AFTER THE ALARM
Although the alarm may have been false,
its mere occurrence sent people running
and consequently muddled the path.
We may not be thinking clearly at the
moment. Best to wait until we regain
our perspicacity.

FIFTH

THE ALARM ALTERNATES
It starts and stops and starts and stops.
Perhaps it is trying to tell us something?
There are matters we have been ignoring
that require our attention.

SIXTH

THE NEIGHBORS' ALARM
The alarm rings down the street and
our neighbors experience unforeseen
trouble. Best to stay in the home and
take no action until this has passed,
lest we become unnecessarily involved.
Marriage causes gossip.

ALL SIX

ACCEPTING THE ALARM
The alarm rings; we listen and take care.
If we follow conventions, then we shall
be free from harm.

*"Where one does not look,
neither are they seen."*

THE SILENCE

STILLNESS

Endless Mountain

Being motionless and without sound is favored at this juncture. He cultivates his meditation and turns his eye inward. It is good to be among people, but best not to notice them or pay them attention. Our energy shall be concentrated on bringing all affairs to a graceful and joyful conclusion. There will be a time for action, but now is the time for silence.

FIRST

A SIMPLE SILENCE
Nothing to say, nowhere to go, nothing
to do; yet we remain joyful. Simplify
and relish the silence.

SECOND

A TARDY SILENCE
He wanted to find silence and stop, but
the decision came after the vehicle had
been set rolling. His heart laments, for
some may have been left behind.

THIRD

SILENCE IN THE LOINS
He wants to be so holy and quash all his
desires, but is not yet advanced enough to
undertake this. This (sexual) tension burns
him away and suffocates his heart. Perhaps
it is better at this time to satisfy our desires:
to do otherwise would be unhealthy.

FOURTH

A HEALTHY SILENCE
He ceases everything: action, desire and
mind. This is healthy and correct at the
present time, for we were well prepared
for such a thing.

FIFTH

SILENCING THE WORDS
He who says less is heard more clearly.
He who says nothing is understood
completely.

SIXTH **SILENT LIKE THE MOUNTAIN**
The song of silence rings through the air
as they realize that they are both staring
at the same spot on the ceiling.

ALL SIX **TRANSCENDING THE SILENCE**
Everything will have its end, even the
silence. Prepare to go forth. Slowly
but surely.

"From far away, that which is large sometimes looks small."

THE SEEKER

THE BRIDE

A Tree upon the Mountain

Just as the river reaches for the ocean, and the ocean
is pulled by the moon, so the seeker is one who flies
toward the sun. As a bride submits to her husband
on her wedding night, the seeker submits to his goal
with devoted and fiercely focused will. By making
progress step by step and by holding onto unwavering
determination, we shall attain what we seek.

漸 THE SEEKER

FIRST

THE SEEKER IN THE OPEN
He does not conceal his actions well, while
neighbors engage in unnecessary gossip.
Someone may be in a certain amount of
trouble, but it is best to turn attention
away from them for the moment.

SECOND

THE SEEKER'S WINE
Although this is not his ultimate
destination, the seeker comes across a
celebration with good wine and good
people. Perhaps it would be good to stay
for a while and enjoy the simple pleasures.

THIRD

THE SEEKER IS LOST
He ventures into the forest and does not
return. The wife is pregnant, but the
child will not come. Everything is going
wrong at the present moment. The oracle
recommends that it is time to direct our
anger at one who is acting unjustly.

FOURTH

THE SEEKER FINDS KINDNESS
Although this is not the ultimate recourse,
the seeker rests under the branches of
a shady tree. We will find a person or
situation that betokens nothing for us but
honorable kindness. For this, we should
be grateful.

FIFTH

THE SEEKER ATTAINS

The river empties into the sea as the
seeker touches the sought and they
become one. That which was willed will
be attained and perhaps a little more.

SIXTH

THE SEEKER NO LONGER

When the river reaches the sea, it ceases
to be, adding to the majesty of the ocean;
and when something touches the sun, it
is consumed by fire, adding to the heat
or perhaps becoming the sun itself. Now
the seeker has ceased to be, and therefore
should be sacrificed to consummate the
power of the One. The wise man sacrifices
what is no longer needed.

ALL SIX

HAUNTING THE SEEKER

Cycles continue to repeat themselves
and he is really going nowhere. There
are things unseen at work. Perhaps it is
time to break from this routine and try
something completely new. Perhaps
embark on a journey?

"In the beginning,
be mindful of the end."

54

THE SERVANT

BOWING

Thunder on the Lake

Entering into service, he forgoes his own wishes to
fulfill the duties of his lord. Nothing much can be
accomplished for ourselves at the present moment,
as our energies are entangled in serving another's
objective. Best to forget ourselves for now, as this
signifies the end of one era and the beginning of
another. The wise man, understanding the tides of
creation, bows his head humbly and accomplishes
the tasks assigned.

歸妹 THE SERVANT

FIRST

ENTERING INTO SERVICE
The young maiden humbly approaches her
new husband, understanding the duties
she must perform. By forgetting ourselves
and serving another, we are able to heal
wounds that would not heal earlier because
we paid them too much attention.

SECOND

THE DAILY SERVICE
Going about daily chores will bring
expected results. If we water the plants,
they will grow. This is nothing special
and seems so simple to understand.

THIRD

THE SERVANT IS PROMOTED
From a bottle washer to a chef: a small
advance is won. This is nothing too
special, but then again, each step is part
of the whole pattern.

FOURTH

WAITING TO ENTER SERVICE
While everybody else positioned
themselves for the good jobs, he frolicked
in the fields and danced in the moonlight.
This was actually a good thing, for he
was not yet emotionally ready to advance.
However, after a certain waiting period, it
is advised to take action and enter service.

FIFTH

THE HUMBLE SERVANT
The first rule is this: Never outshine the master. Even though he had a spark in his eye, he dressed in humble attire to avoid gaining the attention that was meant for his lord. This is a strategic move, for the wise man never lets himself be noticed until ships have already sailed.

SIXTH

THE USELESS SERVANT
He carries a basket to feign work, but there is nothing inside. He stabs at the sheep, but the knife is too blunt to draw blood. There is really nothing to do and nowhere to go. Best to lie low and avoid notice.

ALL SIX

THE SERVANT OVERTAKES
Many a long time observing, contemplating and wiping his lazy lord's chin has led the servant to a deadly understanding of his master's affairs. That said, now is the time to use this knowledge to engage in an uprising and seize power while the lord is in a drunken stupor.

"*Actual abundance may be brief,
yet impressions may outlive stone.*"

THE SUN

SPLENDOR

Thunder and Lightning

The sun rises to the top of the sky in noontime splendor. Now is the time not to be sad, but to shine with all our light blazing forth. If inspiration is required, then it should be sought; if it is in abundance, then it should be given away. Be like the sun, full of strength and there for all. We are One, we are master. The wise man will remember the tides of creation and recognize that nothing lasts forever. That said, after reaching its peak, the sun begins a slow downward progress. We must store this heat in our body for the encroaching dusk.

 THE SUN

FIRST

AN EQUAL SUN
He meets someone of equal rank. It would
be wise to accept their hospitality for
ten days to cultivate respect. However,
anything longer than ten days would
not be good, for destinies would soon
get intertwined.

SECOND

THE ECLIPSED SUN
Something is blocking the heat of the sun
and we are unable to gather the energy
needed to advance. Best to wait until we are
strong, lest we create mistrust. Be content,
for this blockage will not last for long.

THIRD

THE CLOUDED SUN
The rain will not cease and the wood is
beginning to rot. We have been depending
on someone to assist us, but now we
discover them to be quite useless. Better
to do the job ourselves.

FOURTH

UNCOVERING THE SUN
There seems to be so much darkness,
and all seems lost. We should wait until
an equal appears to help us. With the aid
of this helper, we will be able to push
through to the light.

FIFTH

RAYS OF THE SUN

After the storm, rays of healing light appear through the clouds and give the sky a palette of magnificent colors. He steps forth onto the mountain, absorbing this majesty, acquiring unmerited fame and the people's respect.

SIXTH

THE LONELY SUN

Such a magnificent house, but nobody to share it with. He looks out through the gates and sees beautiful forest for miles around, but still he must eat alone and mutter to himself. This is probably our own fault, for we have deliberately isolated ourselves. This will continue for three years. Is the situation acceptable?

ALL SIX

EXAMINING THE SUN

We have done well, but there may be an unseen threat that lies at the root of everything. Best now to analyze things down to their finest detail to uncover this danger.

"He passes like brushfire with courtesy and swiftness."

THE TRAVELER

SWIFTNESS

Fire on the Mountain

Long-distance runner, why are you standing there? The traveler is persistent, stubborn and patient, and will find success in simple matters. Traveling does not serve some great goal, but rather creates simple enjoyment and enough gain to subsidize more traveling. The traveler is spontaneous in his decisions, going where the wind may blow; but he maintains a watchful eye behind that glorious smile. He will have nothing to fear, for it is well known that the Heavens will protect the traveler – the one who forever seeks nothing.

旅 THE TRAVELER

FIRST

THE TRAVELER DISTRACTED
His attention drawn by useless trifles of this or that, his guard is let down and he steps into disaster. The wise man first confronts the important decisions, leaving trifling things for later.

SECOND

THE TRAVELER'S INN
He reaches a safe haven with all his valuables still intact. He is attended by a young servant. We should expect to reach our destination and win a new friend.

THIRD

THE CARELESS TRAVELER
He left a candle alight and burnt down the inn! Now he no longer has a young friend. Although we may be tired, we must still exert caution and take care to clean up our messes.

FOURTH

THE TRAVELER'S BANKROLL
He reaches a stop in which he obtains the money required to finance his trip. However, his heart remains sad for he is unable to attain what he seeks.

FIFTH

THE TRAVELER'S BOUNCE
He falls down one step, but bounces back
two. That is to say, a small loss in the near
future will be advantageous for it will win
us assistance from above.

SIXTH

THE TRAVELER'S KARMA
Someone else experiences misfortune and
the traveler laughs wildly. This is until
he realizes that it affects him as well. He
should have had more respect. What has
been lost will never be recovered.

ALL SIX

THE TRAVELER CELEBRATES
Taking the time to forget about this or
that, the traveler sets down his pack and
uncorks a bottle of red wine to drink with
his new-found friend.

*"Penetrating through the cracks,
gentleness shall carry words afar."*

57

PRAYER

SUBMISSION

A Favorable Wind

Prostrating himself before the altar, he submits himself
to the will of Heaven. For those who are not religiously
inclined, prayer can be taken as a willing submission
to a stronger force, much as a woman opens her womb
and allows seed to penetrate. Prayer can also mean "to
hope" or to let our actions be guided by another, as this
is stronger than carrying on alone. We should have a
goal or precise request when we pray, and it is advised
to take counsel from a wise elder.

PRATER

FIRST

THE SCATTERED PRAYER
He is not sure whether to stand up or
kneel. He is very doubtful about the
course of his actions. However, if he
should rediscover his center and charge
like a tiger, then all shall be well.

SECOND

PRAYERS FROM LEFT FIELD
He thinks himself so broken and shamed
by what has transpired that he crawls
under the bed to hide from the light.
During this time, he employs a rabble of
diviners, wizards, thieves and confidence
men to enact his prayers. And the funny
thing is that it actually works!

THIRD

PRAYERS EXHAUSTED
He prays all through the day, into the
night and even past the dawn, and still
nothing. Prayer is generally a good thing,
but perhaps our willpower has been
exhausted.

FOURTH

THE REWARDS OF PRAYER
He prays for success in hunting deer, but
while in the field spots deer, buffalo and
pheasant. Our prayer is good and has
presented us with new and interesting
opportunities for us to consider.

FIFTH

OPPORTUNITY FROM PRAYER
A small effort at the right time is much more effective than a large effort at the wrong time. That said, there is a major change coming and we should use the six-day opportunity of three before and three after to make our advances. For this is when our power is at its height.

SIXTH

BEGGING MORE THAN PRAYING
Exhausted by constant failure, he crawls under the bed to hide from the light. During this time he continues to pray, but now it sounds more like begging. By doing this, he will lose even his pocket money. Perhaps it is now best to stop praying and start working.

ALL SIX

THE PRAYER TURNED INWARD
Instead of focusing on external things, perhaps it is best to be content with our lot and turn our energies inward.

*"Song, replenishment,
rest and rejoicing."*

58

THE PIPER

SONG

A Crystal Lake

The piper sings his song and marches around, lifting the people with the simple joy of his music. Now is the time to be happy, to sing and to dance. By doing so, we will forget that we even had troubles in the first place. The past is dead, tomorrow is still a dream, today we must make merry! The wise man chants an inspiring tune, raising people's hearts for miles around.

 THE PIPER

FIRST

THE PIPER PLAYS
Singing with confidence, his music is in
harmony. We should act with no doubt:
if there is doubt, then we should not act.

SECOND

THE PIPER MARCHES
Marching forth with confidence, the
people follow his lead and dance in the
streets. The wise man leads by creating
happiness in the hearts of others.

THIRD

THE PIPER TUNES
They were expecting a song, but he must
take time to tune his instrument. What we
have expected will not materialize just yet,
as there is a problem with one of the tools
we employ.

FOURTH

THE PIPER COMPOSES
Instead of playing for the people, the
piper isolates himself to compose a new
tune. This makes him restless yet happy.
Although it may be troublesome to
withdraw for a while, we may wish to
stop and draw up a concrete plan.

FIFTH

THE OBTUSE PIPER
The joy is gone, the people are tired,
and he is singing out of tune. It would be
wise to recognize what is now ending and
to let it go. To be stubborn and carry on
will just bring more trouble and possibly
ensure that we are not invited back.

SIXTH

THE IRRESISTIBLE PIPER
In the moonlight, he looks so irresistible
and makes the women swoon. However,
if they meet him by day on the road,
then things will be different. There is
a superficial attraction, which when
examined will be found to be without
substance.

ALL SIX

THE PIPER'S EAR
Music is a true blessing in life only if we
know how to listen. Perhaps we should
now stop playing and, rather, listen to the
song that sings deep within our heart?

"Distribution, dispersion, sacrifice and perseverance."

THE SHIP

DISPERSING

Wind across Water

Having finished his business on the land, the king invests his resources into constructing seven fine ships to scatter across the seas. This is the time to take what was once One and convert it to the many. It is the time to give freely. It is the time for lightening the load and making sacrifices. It is also the time when travel would be fruitful. The wise man floats through the crowd, dispersing coins to rich and poor alike.

渙　THE SHIP

FIRST **BUILDING THE SHIP**
They come together to accomplish
by means of the many that which was
impossible for the One. We should assist
with the strength of a work horse.

SECOND **THE SHIP'S ALTAR**
Sailing on the high seas, the ship
encounters a storm. He hastens to the altar
to make the correct sacrifices. In the face of
trouble, we should take the "spiritual" or
"moral" stance to confront the adversary.

THIRD **MAINTAINING THE SHIP**
By focusing his energies on the daily
routines of the ship, he finds solace
and soon forgets his own problems. By
focusing on some work that is greater than
ourselves, we will find that everything falls
into accord.

FOURTH **THE SHIP'S CREW**
They do an exemplary job, but he finds
that he can run the ship by himself.
That said, he disperses them in the four
directions to carry on good works in his
name. We should not be afraid of letting
go of something valuable, for in the end
this shall bring us even more wealth.

FIFTH

THE SHIP UNLOADS

It was so laden with cargo that it almost went down at sea. Best to sail to port and relieve this weight – which might be an illness or an emotional burden. Best to let it go by communicating with different people and dispersing it to one hundred different receptacles so that it will harm no one.

SIXTH

THE WAR SHIP

There are reports of pirates at sea, so it is best to equip the ship with a cannon. The mere presence of weapons will offer deterrence enough: we may never have to use them.

ALL SIX

THE SHIP COMES HOME

The time of the sailor is now over. It is recommended that we find a place that we love and throw our energy into creating a stable foundation.

*"Limitations self-imposed,
measuring the vastness."*

60

THE DAM

HOLDING BACK

Water Restrained

By natural instinct, the water wants to flow; however, we must consider the fate of the village below. This is a time to practice restraint, to wait before taking action, or we may set off a chain of events not to our liking. By engaging in restraint, we shall lose nothing, as this is set down for us in the tides of creation. The wise man knows there is a time for both action and non-action. However, we should not hold back to the point where it causes us pain, for this would just lead to a flood.

 THE DAM

FIRST

THE DAM HOLDS
Knowing that action would further
nothing at the moment, he sits on his
porch and sips tea. He will know when
it is the correct time to act, for a path
will open in his mind.

SECOND

MISUSING THE DAM
The crops need to be watered, but he
neglects this and stays at home. We must
take advantage of this opportunity, for it
will soon pass.

THIRD

THE DAM SPILLS
Although he tried to engage in restraint,
things were put into motion regardless.
This is fine and we should allow events
to run their course.

FOURTH

THE DAM CALMS
The water level is low and exerts no
pressure upon the walls. We should enjoy
this moment of peace and continue to
do nothing.

FIFTH

THE DAM'S GATE
Out of respect for our neighbors we have
engaged in voluntary restraint. This was
a good thing. However, now is the time
slowly to open the floodgate and begin
to take action.

SIXTH

THE DAM IS PRESSURED
The water is rapidly rising and the
pressure is causing us much pain. If we
continue like this, then we shall suffer
injury. We should go somewhere or take
action, although do not expect significant
success.

ALL SIX

THE CRUMBLING DAM
The stone is old and the dam springs leaks.
If this continues, then disaster will strike.
Now is the time for success or failure.
Take a risk: if we dare not then we will
lose regardless.

*"Thoughtful in judgment,
justice is forgiveness."*

THE FALCON

SINCERITY

Wind across the Lake

Forever confident and sincere, the falcon is respected by all in the air as the dolphin is in the sea. Sharing the qualities of a king, the falcon urges us to be thoughtful and lenient in our judgments and to radiate outward through the subtle smile of simple and hidden knowledge. The falcon advises us to take a trip or make a change, but to do so lightly, without the burdensome weight of too much baggage. The falcon tells us that it is well to be free, but to remember our nest.

中孚 THE FALCON

FIRST

THE FALCON'S FRIEND
He would perch on the ranger's shoulder,
but when others are around is nowhere
to be seen. Perhaps somebody needs to
be dealt with on a personal basis.

SECOND

THE FALCON'S SONG
He sings it in the shade as the little
birds follow suit. There is a burning
and an honorable longing to share in the
joy of others. If the matter is approached
with sincerity, then all shall go well.

THIRD

THE FALCON'S NEMESIS
The bird down the street just has no
respect. He has made an enemy and is
not sure what to do about it, and now
just runs around in circles. Perhaps
more courage is required?

FOURTH

THE FALCON RISES
Right before the full moon, he gains
inspiration and veers off his present
course. This is the correct decision that
will serve to separate us from the flock.

FIFTH

THE FALCON'S WIND
The wind blows true and carries him
over the hills and through the trees.
Have confidence: if there is wind, then
we should ride it; if there is no wind, row.

SIXTH

THE FALCON'S BOAST
Instead of moving on, he stops to boast
about his good fortune. Sadly, during this
time, the opportunity has passed and he
can move forward no longer. Take care
at the sound of a rooster; if this is heard,
then all should be stopped immediately.

ALL SIX

THE FALCON'S NEST
He already has everything he needs. This
constant soaring through the air has drawn
the attention of the hunter. Better to
retreat to our nest until our impression
has faded from others' minds.

*"Distant thunder makes the
slightest sound. Muted progress
is recommended."*

THE MOUSE

THE CLEVER

Thunder on the Mountain

The mouse is quite the clever creature, skirting around the floor, collecting tidbits for nourishment as larger creatures go hungry. Now is the time to emulate the mouse and not attempt great things. For when a bird flies too high, its singing is out of tune. This is the time to be humble, thrifty, and simple in action and word. There will be a time for greatness, but for the moment we are advised to be small and clever like the mouse.

小過 THE MOUSE

FIRST

THE BIRD AND THE MOUSE
The bird flies high and finds only
misfortune, while the mouse stays on the
ground and continues to survive. If we
try to be like the bird, then we will fail.

SECOND

THE MOUSE'S MOTHER
Although he sought the father, he actually
encountered the mother, who had a word
or two for him. Whether this is good or
not is a personal judgment.

THIRD

THE MOUSE'S NEMESIS
Someone under our care is jealous of our
power and plotting in the shadows to cause
our undoing. The wise man recognizes this
danger and takes the correct precautions.

FOURTH

THE MIGHTY MOUSE
Instead of skulking in the shadows, he
accosts his adversary and draws unneeded
trouble to himself. Now is not the time
for confrontation; rather, it is the time
for success through smallness.

FIFTH

THE DESERT MOUSE

He wanders though the desert searching for water. There are clouds in the west, but they rise too high before they can break. He takes a shot with his bow and hits something other than the intended target. Being too late to seize the presented opportunity, he takes a chance and encounters something unexpected and new. Is this a good thing?

SIXTH

THE PRIDEFUL MOUSE

He had grown so proud of his smallness that when the time came to act, he did nothing. This invites disaster, for someone or something has us in their sights and the only recourse is a direct confrontation.

ALL SIX

THE MOUSE'S CACHE

Winter is coming and it is advised to be frugal and begin to store resources to weather out the storm.

*"The work is finished yet
we must remain vigilant."*

DUSK

AFTERWARD

Water above Fire

The reflective glow of the setting sun spreads across
the land announcing the end of an era. As everything
is virtually finished, small extraneous matters may
be accomplished, but more serious matters will fail,
simply owing to a lack of time or space. The dusk is the
time to accept that things are completed and the work
is done. Enjoy the glow, night is coming.

FIRST

STOPPING AT DUSK

He engages the brake on the wagon and will go no further. This is just as well, for if he had pushed into the night, then he would have encountered bandits.

SECOND

THE VEIL OF DUSK

The veil of dusk drops and suddenly she is exposed in the moonlight. She should not be afraid, for her beauty is a natural thing and should be shared. In seven days, she can return to her family's home. This indicates a seven-day period of mating or potential power. Use it well.

THIRD

CONQUERING THE DUSK

Riding forth into the dusk with no fear of devils, he takes upon himself a righteous cause and devotes three years to its attainment. It will be tiresome, it will be burdensome, but it will succeed.

FOURTH

SHOPPING BY DUSK

One must be wary of making purchases by the glow of the setting sun, for sometimes rags will be mixed in with the silk. Be cautious, for there may be something unforeseen.

FIFTH

THE WINDOW OF DUSK

A small effort with the correct timing
will gain us much more than a large effort
with the incorrect timing. Observe and
capture the opportunity.

SIXTH

THE DUSK OBSCURES

The light had gone and he tripped over a
log, getting his head wet. If he stops and
makes a fire, then all shall be well. This
indicates trouble, but the sort of trouble
for which we know the solution.

ALL SIX

BLACK DUSK

The darkest hour of the night always
comes right before dawn. Expect the most
difficult of times to descend upon us. If we
should persist through those, then relief is
not far behind.

"Glorious is inaction.
Observation is divine."

64

DAWN

BEFORE

Fire above Water

As dawn raised her rosy fingers over the hill, the rooster crowed twice. He knew there was much work to be done. Sadly, it was too early, for the ice had not yet melted and he was unable to complete the crossing. The dawn is a time of silence and beauty, a time to feel alive and absorb the majesty of creation. However, it is not yet the time for forward action. For this, we must wait for the sun.

臨 DAWN

FIRST

SLEEPING PAST DAWN
While he should have been up with the first hints of light, he oversleeps and misses the appointment. He should be ashamed of not taking advantage of such an obvious opportunity.

SECOND

STOPPING FOR DAWN
He was going down the wrong path and the light of dawn illuminated this for him. After stopping and turning, he can start again.

THIRD

DAWN BY THE RIVER
The ice will not permit passage: it must first be melted by the sun. He should wait and watch resolutely for this opportunity and move forward once the way opens up.

FOURTH

CONQUERING THE DAWN
Riding forth into the dawn with no fear of devils, he commits himself to a great cause that will take three years to complete.

FIFTH

ALMS AT DAWN
The monk wanders through the village
at dawn asking the people for his daily
food. The wise man feels honored at the
opportunity to give to such a cause.
Now is the time to be generous.

SIXTH

DRUNK AT DAWN
They drank wine and sang songs until
night turned into day. If this was done
with trustworthy people, then all shall be
well. Just take care not to drink too much,
lest we fall into the river!

ALL SIX

AFTER THE DAWN
Shining in its brilliancy, Father Sun brings
us a realization of the hopes and dreams
we cast at dawn. Love.

The Celestial Dragon I Ching
Neyma Jahan

First published in the UK and USA in 2012 by
Watkins Publishing, an imprint of
Duncan Baird Publishers Ltd
Sixth Floor, Castle House
75–76 Wells Street, London W1T 3QH

Created and designed by Duncan Baird Publishers

Editors: Josephine Bonde and James Hodgson
Designer: Allan Sommerville
Production: Uzma Taj

British Library Cataloguing-in-Publication Data:
A CIP record for this book is available from the British Library

Library of Congress Cataloging-in-Publication Data available

ISBN: 978-1-78028-375-3

10 9 8 7 6 5 4 3 2 1

Typeset in Ehrhardt MT
Printed in China by Imago

Distributed in the USA and Canada by
Sterling Publishing Co., Inc.
387 Park Avenue South
New York, NY 10016-8810

For information about custom editions, special sales, premium and
corporate purchases, please contact Sterling Special Sales Department at
800-805-5489 or specialsales@sterlingpub.com.

		HEAVEN	THUNDER	WATER
HEAVEN		**1** Dragon	**34** Horns	**5** Clouds
THUNDER		**25** Surprise	**51** Alarm	**3** Storm
WATER		**6** Claws	**40** Arrow	**29** Abyss
MOUNTAIN		**33** Hermit	**62** Mouse	**39** Raven
EARTH		**12** Bargain	**16** Hammer	**8** Coven
WIND/WOOD		**44** Gate	**32** Marathon	**48** Well
FIRE		**13** Beloved	**55** Sun	**63** Dusk
LAKE		**10** Razor	**54** Servant	**60** Dam